Papier Mache Art & Design

By Jackie Hall

Papier Mache Art & Design

ISBN 978-0-9560571-0-5

Explore and share: http://www.papiermache.co.uk

2tap Publishing
For bulk purchase requests, contact information or to report errors, please send an e-mail to publishing@2tap.com c/o Russ Hall.

From **2tap Publishing**

Contents

Introduction

I have been working with papier mache for many years and have never ceased to be amazed at the endless possibilities that this simple yet so versatile medium can lead to.

Every day I encounter surprise from people who just don't realise what fantastic results papier mache can give.

You can make papier mache look like almost any other material – wood, metal, porcelain or pottery. It will take practically any paint and varnish you care to use. It is strong, light and inexpensive to make. You won't need to go out and buy lots of expensive materials. You will probably find most things you need in your own home.

In this book, I aim to share with you my experiences and take you though each step in detail to help you to get as much satisfaction from working with papier mache as I have. You will find lots of interesting projects that you can easily interpret to your own design and imagination.

Each project lists what you will need as additions to the basic papier mache requirements which are the same for every project. See "Chapter 2 – How To Make Papier Mache". At the end of each project you will find some suggestions as to how you can adapt the basic idea.

I hope you will get a lot of enjoyment from this book and I hope it will put you on the path to a very rewarding and pleasurable activity.

Have Fun!

Jackie

PAPIER MACHE *Art*

P - Paper, which has been around since time emmorium, is available in abundance in the form of newspapers, magazines, junk mail, office paper and wrapping papers. The ancient Chinese soon realised the potential of waste paper products and turned them into useful items such as warrior's helmets.

Through the ages, functional items such as furniture, toys and interior mouldings for buildings, continued to put paper to good use. Today, we have gone on to products such as plastic so there is no longer the need for paper to be used. However, paper mixed with adhesive (papier mache) is becoming increasingly popular as an art form in this waste conscious world that we now live in. People have more leisure time and want to express themselves and be creative. Papier mache is the ideal medium. It is inexpensive, readily available and easy to use.

A - Art. Papier mache is a wonderful release for artistic expression. It can be moulded and shaped, cut, sawn, sanded and even have more added on to it. It can then be painted, varnished or can be used with other mediums such as mosaic or decoupage.

P - Patience. This is the one skill that you must have to be able to get good results from papier mache. There is virtually no outlay or complicated equipment to get hold of to make a start. You can be as simple or complex as you like in your ideas and as long as you have the patience to wait until your papier mache dries thoroughly, you will be on the right track.

I - Inspiration. This book is intended to give you inspiration and encouragement, rather than simply a book full of projects for you to copy. While these are fun and helpful up to a point, true satisfaction can only come from creating something from within yourself. Look around you at the world. Study the things that interest you, whether it be flowers, animals, people, machines, or a hobby. Look at the things in detail and try to imagine them smaller/larger than life. Isolate a small area of your interest and see what patterns and shapes you see. Use these to fire your imagination. You will soon be full of ideas and bursting to go.

E - Emulsion paint. This common water based household paint really is the key to a successful finished object. Painting a dried papier mache item with a couple of coats, although a rather mundane procedure, is very important in preparation for your artwork. It will not only kill the newsprint, but will give you a "blank canvas" to work on. A bit of time and care sanding between each coat will make all the difference to your end product. Think of it like building the foundations for your house.
You can use up leftover paint from your decorating. It doesn't have to be white, though a pale colour is preferable. If you have to buy it, there is no need to buy top quality, but don't go for the cheapest either, it will give disappointing results. If the paint is very thick you may need to water it down slightly.

R - Research. When you have chosen your subject, look at as many pictures as you can. Decide how big you want your artwork to be and whether you want to make it over an armature or on a base. Will it be made in relief on the side of a large pot or box? You will probably have difficulty in deciding what to do at this stage as you will see that the possibilities are endless.

M - Modelling.
When you make a papier mache pulp mixture, it looks and feels like clay. You can mould it with your fingers and shape it. You can push it into a mould or use it to make relief shapes and patterns on a flat or rounded surface.

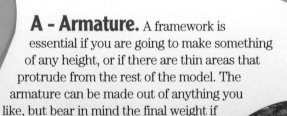

A - Armature. A framework is essential if you are going to make something of any height, or if there are thin areas that protrude from the rest of the model. The armature can be made out of anything you like, but bear in mind the final weight if it is going to be large.

C - Colour. This is artwork you are doing here. Don't be tied to convention. If you want to make a huge blue daffodil, then make a huge blue daffodil! You have all the wonderful colours under the sun at your disposal. Go ahead and use them.

H - Happiness!
The feelings of euphoria you will experience when you have completed a piece of artwork are priceless.

E - Experiment.
If, having decided to make a particular piece, you are unsure how it will work out, then make a maquette. This can be a simple model made of scrunched up kitchen paper, or you could do as I sometimes do and make a small model in plasticine. This is also useful for turning around to see the model from all sides.

A - Approach.
You must believe that you can achieve the results you are expecting – then you will!

R - Right way to do it?
No such thing! There is never a right or a wrong way to do anything in the art world. As long as you stick by the basic common sense stuff like making sure that you don't put too many layers on at once, or paint it before it is completely dry, you can be free to do it **your** way.

T - Try.
You may be surprised what you can achieve!

How to make PAPIER MACHE

Basically, newspaper is all you need. If you want to, there are endless other papers and different adhesives you can use to make your papier mache.

If, however, your aim is to be artistic like me (as opposed to making a durable piece of furniture, for example) the less you have to worry about getting the right ingredients the better. Just as in a recipe, you can decorate and make a beautiful sponge cake easily, so why make a complicated gateaux?

It may seem daft, but there is actually a correct way to tear newspaper! It needs to be torn with the grain (usually across the paper). Try tearing it the other way and you will see what I mean!

Tear the strips to sizes in accordance with what you are making. As a general guide, to cover an average sized balloon, the ideal size is about one inch wide strips by four inches. For larger projects you can use larger pieces. If you were making a life-sized elephant, small strips would take you a lifetime. I tend to use pieces about the size of a quarter of a page of newspaper for really large projects. Again, for very small projects, small strips are needed and even smaller to get around curves and intricate shapes.

At the end of the day though, tear the pieces into the sizes that you feel comfortable working with. Practice will help you find what suits you best. Never cut the newspaper with scissors as the edges will be too sharp and will not lie flat when you press them onto your work. By the same token, you may choose to avoid the edges of the paper.

Put your pile of newspaper strips to one side. It helps to get these ready as once you have started to lay your papier mache your fingers will get very sticky.

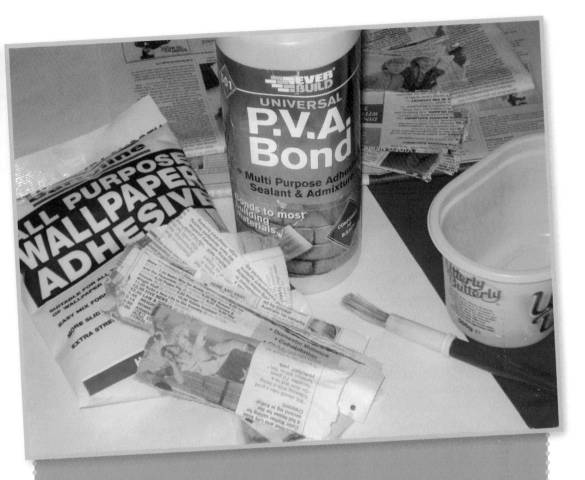

THE ADHESIVE

There are quite a few options to use for your adhesive. In the past, flour and water was often used (as was probably used in your schooldays). Some people still use this today, but I like to use wallpaper paste. It is easily obtained, inexpensive, quick to make up and contains a fungicide to prevent mould. I have used wallpaper paste throughout this book. If you wish to substitute it for another adhesive you still carry out all the procedures just the same.

When mixing your paste, use a plastic or china jug or bowl and fill it with warm water. Leave some room for the paste and allow for stirring. Make the paste as directed by the manufacturer. Always sprinkle the powder into the water (never the other way around) and mix briskly. You may decide to use a little more powder than they suggest to give you a stiffer mix. You will soon get used to the best amount to use.

Adding a small amount of white (pva) glue to the wallpaper paste will help give it extra strength. If you are going to do a lot of papier mache it is economical to buy a big tub of it from a hardware store – go on, treat yourself!

Once your paste is made up, keep it in a cool place if you don't use it all at once. It is a good idea to make up only the amount you require for a day or two to prevent spoiling and wastage. The paste will keep for a few days, but will gradually go watery and lose its stickiness then all you can do is discard it.

PREPARING YOUR WORKSURFACE

It is a good idea to cover your table with a plastic sheet. Pasting can splash a bit and you can simply wipe the sheet clean when you have finished.

A plastic or melamine board is extremely useful to use as a pasting mat. Anything in fact that is smooth and non absorbent. A half inch brush is ideal to use to paste the pieces. Take one strip of paper at a time and lay it on the board. Paste liberally all over the strip. Just like in wallpapering a wall, make sure that every bit is covered. Now turn it over and paste the other side. This will ensure full absorption of the adhesive.

PULP

The other common form of papier mache is pulp. To make pulp, tear up some newspaper (it doesn't have to be in neat strips) and place it in an old saucepan half filled with water.

Put the saucepan onto the stove and bring the water to boiling point. Let it simmer for half an hour to break up the fibres of the paper. An old wooden spoon is ideal for giving it an occasional stir. The printing ink from the newspaper will stain everything it comes into contact with so only use old utensils.

Note: Make sure that there is room in the saucepan to allow for expansion without spilling over the top.

Remove the saucepan from the stove and allow to cool. When it has cooled down, if you have an old liquidiser that you could use, spoon very small amounts into it (with plenty of water) and give it a quick twirl. It is not absolutely essential to do this but it helps to further break up the fibres. Again, don't fill the liquidiser too full and only put in a very small amount of paper pulp at a time.

Finally, sieve the pulp in a surplus kitchen sieve. Lightly press down on the pulp with the back of a wooden spoon, pressing out as much water as you can. You can also extract some of the water by placing a lump in your hand and giving it a light squeeze. Don't be over zealous though, you need to keep some moisture in so that you can mix in your adhesive. When you have thoroughly mixed it with your paste, you are ready to use the pulp as required.

You can see photographs of this process in "Barrel of laughs".

MOULDS AND ARMATURES

The choices open to you are endless. You could lay strips over a balloon or bowl, you could lay them onto a piece of cardboard that you have pre-cut to shape or you could make yourself an armature. The framework can be made out of wire and/or wire netting, cardboard, polystyrene chunks or for smaller areas, just a piece of scrunched up dry newspaper. Hold it all together with masking tape. Don't use sellotape or any other shiny surface tape as the papier mache will not stick to it.

Balloons make excellent moulds. They can be bought in many different sizes and shapes.

To build a wire frame, all you will need is a roll of fencing wire and some wire netting. Get hold of a set of wire cutters and you are all set up. You may also like to buy a roll of very thin wire. You can cut very short lengths of this and use it to "stitch" together the wire and wire netting.

If you are making a large armature it is worthwhile taking a bit of time over the framework. It will save a lot of time and give much better results. Make sure that there is sufficient wire used to hold it all in place once the papier mache is added. Wet papier mache is very heavy indeed and you don't want it to sag under the pressure. Think of it like a skeleton. Making it hollow inside will keep the weight to an absolute minimum, but make sure that any protruding bits are well supported to keep their shape.

Using wire netting is very unkind on your hands, so it is advisable to use gloves when handling it.

You can see examples of this technique in "Large Armatures".

CARDBOARD

For items that require a lot of strength, use corrugated cardboard (the type used to make strong packing boxes). For extra strength, use double corrugated. Thinner cardboard can be used for lighter pieces and card for small areas.

CARDBOARD IS THIRSTY – SEAL IT!

Cardboard drinks moisture like a sponge. Remember that you will be placing very wet strips of paper onto your cardboard. What is it going to do? Get wet, yes – then warp! A papier mache artist's worst nightmare is warping! It can throw your whole artwork out the window.

A very simple solution is to seal your cardboard with some watered down (50/50) pva glue. Make sure every area is covered. Give it two coats if you like to make sure. Once this is dried, which shouldn't take very long, your cardboard will be sealed. The pva glue dries quickly and is fairly water resistant so it won't be too affected by the wet paper strips.

Place the pasted strip on the object that you wish to cover. Lay it down carefully and smooth it over gently but firmly with your fingers and thumbs. Make sure that you have no air bumps trapped underneath. When the strip is secure and perfectly smooth, take your next piece of paper and repeat. Lay the strips in the same direction initially, then lay the next ones in the opposite direction. This will help to give strength to your finished piece.

KNOWING WHEN TO STOP!

Don't be tempted to lay more than a layer or two at any one time. This is not just because of the fact that it will take longer to dry, but also because of the way papier mache responds to moisture. The wetter papier mache is, the more it shrinks. What you may think is saving you time, will actually cost

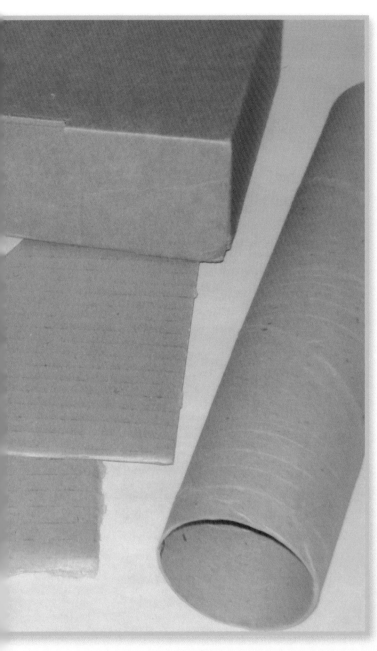

you dearly as the papier mache will distort so much while it is drying, that you will end up with lumps and bumps which will take many layers to put right, if indeed you can ever get it really smooth again. The resulting soggyness will also make it impossible for you to continue smoothing strips down successfully. Putting too many layers on at once will give you a surface resembling the craters on the moon. If however, you want your piece to look like craters on the moon, go ahead! Creating this effect on purpose can be quite dramatic but it won't suit all your work.

You can see some examples of this in "Tulips".

DRYING

When you have finished laying your strips, the object will be moist and vulnerable. Drying can take a long time, so it is a good idea to place the item in front of an electric fan for an hour or two to kick start the drying process. This will make quite a dramatic difference. Cold air blowing from a fan, or placing the item outside in a stiff breeze also freshens the piece up. Avoid heat drying as it can cause distortion.

ALL DRY AND READY TO GO!

Once the whole piece is thoroughly dry (leave it a bit longer even if you think it looks bone dry, just to make sure), paint it with two coats of white emulsion. Sand between coats. When your item is painted all one colour it will look very different. It no longer has the distractive shadings of the newspaper print. This gives you a chance to really study the piece. Anything you don't like about it you can put right at this stage. You can sand it, cut bits off or add more papier mache to build it up.

Leave any additional papier mache to dry thoroughly as before, then touch up these areas with emulsion paint. You can save money by using up leftover tins of emulsion or by buying sample pots if you only require a small amount.

On To The Arty Bit

When you are clued up on the basics of making mache items, you can really start on your art work.

Don't worry if you are not sure how to go about achieving your goal. Just start! If you go wrong (as we all do every so often) you can almost always rectify it with this wonderful medium. If you have made a part too large, cut it down and cover up your mistake with more papier mache. If an area is too small, build it up. If you are not very pleased with the shape something has turned out, make it into something else altogether. You may well find that the finished result isn't at all as you had originally planned, but you could still be delighted with the end result. You may have created something that you would not have thought of doing and everyone will praise you for it. You don't have to let on that you got there by default!

Ideas and inspiration

The more you do, the more ideas you will get. It is rather like sitting down to write a letter. Before you start, you often don't have much idea about what you will write about, but once you have written the first few lines, thoughts flood into your head and you can hardly get everything down on paper quick enough. The same works with art, one thing leads to another and you will lead off at different tangents and surprise yourself at what you can come up with.

How to decorate

There are endless ways to decorate your work. Paint effects and embellishments can transform the most ordinary piece of papier mache into a masterpiece.

Use a soft pencil to draw your design or patterns onto the white painted surface of your work as a guide.

If you are going to decorate your work with coloured paper, there is no need to paint with emulsion paint first, unless you want to do it as a means of showing up any discrepancies.

Painting techniques

When painting colours, bear in mind that they tend to dry very slightly darker than they appear in the wet form, just as happens when you paint the walls in your living room.

Acrylic paints are ideal for painting papier mache. They are water based and dry very quickly. Some of the metallic colours look stunning and its sometimes hard see the difference between the papier mache and the real thing.

Copper

Here I have used copper acylic paint to cover the letter C. To make the rivets, I glued some jewellery findings onto the papier mache before laying the strips over the top. Not all embellishments need to be seen – they can still make an impression!

Granite

This hard stone colour suited the heavy, sharp cornered letter E. It looks as though it would be really heavy to pick up!

Pewter

Here I used silver metallic paint. When the paint was thoroughly dry, I dry-brushed some black ink over it. This has given a pewter effect.

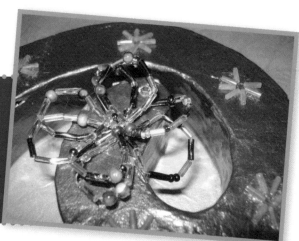

Metallic paint

You can buy several colours with a metallic finish. This 'e' has been painted and then varnished with a high gloss varnish. I have added beads and gems to the finished surface.

Marble

To get a marble effect, paint all one colour and leave to dry. Using two or three slightly lighter/darker colours, merge in some sweeps of paint across the area (in one direction) to represent natural rock layers.

When dry, with a dark colour paint and a very thin brush, paint some veins in a different direction to the first. Varnish with a satin or matt varnish.

Dripping candle wax

You can achieve a dripping candle wax effect by first painting your work one colour and leaving to dry.

Taking just one colour paint at a time, liberally pour the paint onto the top of the work and let it run down the sides. Do this with several different colours, but make sure that each colour is dry before adding the next. Brush with a few coats of varnish when completely dry to protect the raised paint from flaking off.

Decoupage

Papier mache looks as attractive as wood covered in decoupage. It just needs a good sanding first to get it smooth.

Decoupage is the art of gluing cut out pictures onto an object, then covering with many layers of varnish until you have a smooth surface.

Collect some pictures from magazines or wrapping paper and carefully cut them out. Paint a base colour on your papier mache and arrange your pictures. Don't use glue at this stage. Move the pieces around until you are happy with the arrangement. Glue them in place with diluted pva glue. Make sure that they are smoothed down and fully stuck.

When dry, varnish with several coats of varnish, letting each layer dry in between. After the 4th layer, give it a very light sanding with fine sandpaper before adding the next coat, then after each layer thereafter.

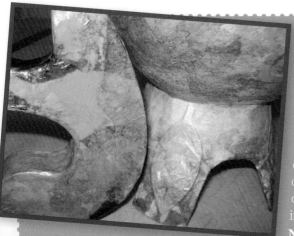

Tissue covered

Coloured tissue paper covering papier mache gives it a very subtle, delicate finish. You can paint a base colour on first if you like, or just leave it white. You can use just one colour of tissue paper or several different colours overlapping. As tissue is so fine, the colours will show through the pieces overlapping them which can create an interesting look.

Note: When using tissue, bear in mind that it is a very fragile paper which will break up easily when wet. The colours may run; you could end up with stained fingers! If you don't want the colour to run, make sure you buy a non-running type of tissue paper.

The best way to fix tissue onto your work, is to paste the work itself, rather than the tissue. Brush your paste over the whole area you want to cover and carefully lay each piece of torn tissue onto it. Smooth each piece down with the paste brush. I used diluted 50/50 pva glue.

To protect your work, you can brush it with more of the diluted pva glue as I have done here. It looks natural and has a nice soft sheen.

Embellishments
Many items can be glued onto your work to enhance its appearance.

Mosaic/Mirrors

You can use mosaic tiles on your work, or as I have done here, tiny glass mirrors. I actually got these mirrors by dissecting a large Christmas bauble! I varnished the piece before gluing the mirrors on.

Glass nuggets

These glass nuggets are freely available to buy and not too expensive. They can sometimes be found in florist shops. One or two glued onto your work can look stunning.

Sand/Packing paper

Here I have laid a trail of glue and sprinkled sand onto it. The top has some zig-zaggy type packing paper that I received a gift in.

Beads

All kinds of beads can be used. The flatter ones can be glued down and others can be strung into shapes and threaded through your work.

To fix the strung beads to the letter 'e' I used an awl to make a hole for the wires to sit in and glued it into place.

Undercover work

There are lots of objects you can place beneath your paper strips. Have a rummage around your home and you will find all sorts of things that you can use. Here are some examples:

String

String is excellent for forming lines and squiggles. Simply glue a line or swirl onto your work and carefully lay a length of string along the glue line. When the glue is dry you can papier mache over the top, smoothing the pieces around the string. This will achieve a lovely raised surface. When you are painting you can pick out this raised area in a different colour.

Jewellery findings

Have a look in your jewellery box for broken pieces of jewellery. The findings make excellent patterns when covered over in papier mache. Buttons too can be used.

Surface effects

Uneven surface

Using pulp as your final layer (you can use layered strips first, then top coat with a thin layer of pulp), it will give you an uneven surface which adds drama to your painting.

Skin deep

The most natural looking skin can be made with toilet paper! Broken down in water and mixed with pva glue it gives an almost porcelain finish.

Here I will show you how to make realistic looking skin:

Place some boiling water from a kettle into a large pan or bowl. Tear off some sheets of white toilet paper and drop them into the water. Stir with an old wooden spoon.

Add some skin coloured acrylic paint to the pulp. If you add the colour at this stage it soaks into the paper and gives a more natural finish.

Sieve the pulp over a jug or bowl.

Press down on the pulp with the wooden spoon and place the pulp in a bowl. Add enough pva glue to make a nice workable consistency then apply the pulp to the item you wish to cover.

This pulp only needs to be spread thinly, but deep enough to completely cover your work.

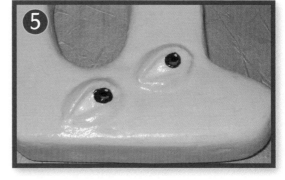

Leave to dry. This will take what seems like a lifetime to dry, but don't worry, it will dry out eventually! For the first day or two it will look exactly the same. It could take anything up to a week to dry out completely so you can't be in a rush if you use this method.

When it is dry, the next bit is nothing less than sheer hard work! You will need to sand it with sandpaper like you have never sanded anything before. If you get most of it nice and smooth, but there is still a few tiny gaps, you can add a little plaster or filler, coloured with the same paint you used for the pulp. It is much better though if you don't use it. The results really pay off in the end – I promise!

A couple of coats of diluted pva glue to seal it and there you have it – very natural looking skin.

Tools/Tricks of the trade

Brushes
There is no need to buy expensive artist's brushes, but they do need to be of a good enough quality to prevent hairs from falling out during painting. The surface of papier mache can be quite tough on paintbrushes. Where possible, try to keep brushes used for paint separate from those used for varnishes/sealers. This will prevent tiny dried bits of paint being released from the brush head spoiling your clear finish. In any case, make sure they are cleaned thoroughly after use. It is also a good idea to keep two separate pots of turps if you are using oil based paints so that one does not contaminate the other.

White (pva) glue
There are several types of white glue, ranging from the weakest and cheapest (as you might find in a toyshop) to strong ones that are used in strengthening concrete. The best type of pva for papier mache work is somewhere in the middle. It is worth buying a good quality, but there is no need to go into the very expensive brands either.

Decorating the inside of your work
Where you are covering an item such as a bowl, balloon etc, one way to deal with the inside is to use coloured paper for your first layer. You then resort to newspaper strips until your final layer then you return to your coloured paper. This way the total of the outside and inside will be covered in the same paper and there will be no need to paint or paper the inside.

You can find an example of pasting the inside of your work in "Barrel of laughs".

Where am I going wrong? Try taking a photograph of your work. This will often show up the problems. Sometimes simply holding it up to a mirror will do the same job.

TULIPS

Starter Tutorial

T his is a starter tutorial to give you the general idea how to make an attractive papier mache item using the simple layering method covering a balloon.

The same basic principles will apply to everything else that you make. I chose my tulips to demonstrate the technique because of their popularity on my site and for the benefit of all those people that have asked me to give them detailed instructions on how to make them.

Layering method of papier mache

This project uses the basic layering method of papier mache. This method applies to whatever you are making. First, tear the newspaper into strips approximately an inch wide by 4 inches long.

Make up some wallpaper paste in a bowl, adding a little less water than recommended by the manufacturer. You need thick glue to make a strong bonding agent. Add some white (pva) glue to give it added strength.

Taking one piece of paper at a time, paste both sides evenly with the brush and place over the object you wish to cover. Press down lightly but firmly, taking care to smooth out any air bubbles. Cover the whole object with 1 or 2 layers of strips, overlapping them as you do so. Leave in an airy place to dry.

When completely dry, continue to build up 1 or 2 layers at a time until you have the required thickness.

You will need:

- ❖ Small round balloon
- ❖ Newspaper
- ❖ Wallpaper paste
- ❖ White (pva) glue
- ❖ Bowl to mix the paste in
- ❖ Flat paintbrush
- ❖ Strong scissors
- ❖ Masking tape
- ❖ Thick cardboard
- ❖ Thin card
- ❖ Glue
- ❖ Black marker pen
- ❖ White emulsion paint
- ❖ Polyfilla (1 cup) (optional)
- ❖ Paint
- ❖ Polyurethane varnish
- ❖ Plastic bottle or jar (optional)

Step by step

Blow up the balloon and knot tightly. Paste strips all around the balloon excluding the area around the knot. Cover with 1 or 2 layers. Tie a piece of string around the knot and hang it up to dry.

Tip: Drying papier mache over a balloon:

You must be very careful in the drying process. Make sure you do not leave it longer than 24 hours before adding the next strips. You want the papier mache to dry as quickly as possible, but you must not put the balloon anywhere where the temperature is different from where you pasted it.

I am a great believer in the electric fan to dry things, but in the case of a balloon, it is not advisable. The cool air from the fan will cool the air inside the balloon, making it deflate slightly. This will lead to ghastly creases forming which you don't want! When completely dry, cover with another 1/2 layers of strips. Again leave to dry.

This is an example of working too slowly. Not enough layers have been built up before the balloon started to deflate. The result is a weak shell that will collapse in the first puff of wind!

Chapter 4

Repeat the process for a third or fourth time to give you a strong mould. Again, don't leave it longer than 24 hours. The balloon inside will only stay firm long enough to keep its shape for a very limited time. Although this may not show up when you first pick up your balloon, as soon as you start adding more strips, the dry layers beneath will soon become saturated and start to wrinkle. It will be impossible for you to put any pressure on the strips to get a nice smooth finish. Before long, the original layers will be so distorted that you will not be able to continue with it.

The same thing will happen if you try to add too many layers at once. The papier mache will get so saturated that it will disfigure. So stick to little and often, so that you can build up many layers in as short a time as possible. Once you have the required thickness on your balloon, the panic is over and you can leave it as long as you like. This is the key to achieving that super smooth finish.

This is an example of too many layers added at one time. The vast volume of liquid in the layers has disfigured the shape.

①

Cut a circle of thick cardboard for the base. Put a blob of glue right in the centre and place your covered balloon on top. The underside of the balloon will be curved, so this will provide a flat base for your vase. To secure the covered balloon to the cardboard, coat some larger pieces of newspaper with paste and scrunch them up. Wedge these pieces in between the cardboard and your vase shape. Leave to stand until the glue has set.

Continue pressing in scrunched up paper until you have brought the sides almost level with the outer edges of the cardboard. Leave to dry thoroughly.

When completely dry (this may take quite a while because of the thickness of the layers of paper), put more strips of paper over the base and just up the sides to give a smooth finish.

Tip: It may help to brush some paste onto the scrunched area first to ensure ample adhesion of the new strips.

Burst the balloon and remove. Paint the rim of the vase with white emulsion. This will make it easier to mark where you need to make cut-outs. Cut the opening with strong scissors to an even height. Divide the top into roughly three equal parts and draw three petals with a black marker pen.

④

⑤

Cut out the three petals with a pair of scissors. You will now have your three inner petals.

⑥

From 3 pieces of thin card (slightly longer than the height of the tulip) cut out your three outer petals.

Bend each petal into a curved shape, taping the join with masking tape.

You will now need to attach the three outer petals to the main tulip body. This is the trickiest part and needs a bit of care and patience!

Each petal needs to be lined up with the "gap" in between the original ones. Try to make sure that they are equally spaced around the outside. They need to be stuck down and then taped into place. You may find it helpful to put a blob of fast drying glue onto the bottom of the inside of each petal to fix them in place quickly, allowing you to get them lined up properly.

Using small pieces of masking tape, carefully fix down all the sides of the petals. Some card might be sticking out below the base after you have adjusted the petals into position. Just trim these pieces of card with a pair of scissors and tape the bottom edges just like the sides.

Note: Don't panic if some of your petals are not a perfect fit. Balloons vary in size so you might have to adjust the curve of some of the petals. You can do this by making a snip, as you would do when wallpapering, and join with more masking tape. Papier Mache covers a multitude of sins!

You are now ready to papier mache over the whole tulip. Cover both the inside and the outside of each petal you have added. Again, only a couple of layers at a time. You no longer have to worry about a balloon deflating so you can take your time in between layering sessions.

There is no need to put more papier mache on the inner petals as these will be strong enough already. However, you do need to put some strips over the edges where you cut them, in order to seal them and make a smoother edge.

Build up the layers on the outer petals, taking the strips to the outer edges and overlapping them a little onto the inner petals and base.

While the petals are wet and pliable, bend them a little to add realism and leave to dry.

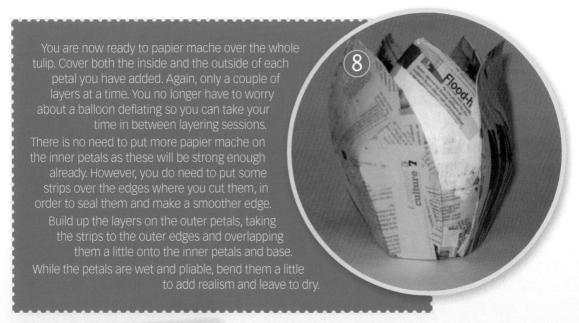

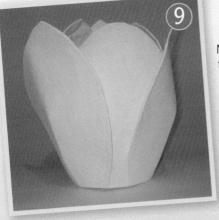

Now the tulip is finished, you need to paint it with two coats of white emulsion paint. (It doesn't have to be white, but a pale colour is best). This is to seal your papier mache and it will also show up anything that is glaringly wrong and give you the chance to correct it (by maybe sanding, bending or adding more papier mache to the area).

Using the paint of your choice (I've used acrylic paint), put a base coat of colour on your tulip. You may need a second coat according to the type of paint you are using.

Using a selection of alternative colours, add flecks of paint to the petals, paying particular attention to the tips and the outside fold. This can be done in one of two ways, or a combination of both. Place your colours in a dish and using your brush, pick up small amounts of one and then another colour. Smudge these brush strokes into each other. This is best done at the same time while all the paint is wet.

When the paint has dried, have a good look at it and using dry brush stokes (this is where you put some paint on your brush, then wipe most of it off onto a piece of kitchen paper, then quickly and lightly brush this over the surface). This will merge any colours that you are not happy about.

Using different colours helps to add realism to your flower. Even on a flower which is one coloured, there are enormous variations in colour shading if you look closely enough.

Finally, 2 or three coats of polyurethane varnish will seal your tulip and enhance the colours. I've used satin finish.

If you want to turn your tulip into a vase, you will need to make a flat surface inside to stand a water container on.

To do this, mix up a cup full of polyfilla (pouring consistency) and pour it into the vase. This will also act as a weight to help keep your vase stable.

Cut down an empty squash bottle or similar container to hold water and stand this inside the tulip.

I have now taken you through all the stages in making a tulip. You will see as you go through my book that this basic technique is what I have used for many different projects. The possibilities are endless once you have mastered the simple steps. You can keep referring back to this tutorial if you need any help.

You can make these tulips any size you like. Just remember to keep the bases and petals in proportion.

Chapter 5

ROSE
Bud

As an alternative to the tulip, a beautiful rosebud can be made. Follow the same basic instructions for the tulip until you get to the petal stage. The tops of rose petals are square shaped with rounded corners. You will need to cut three petals out of the basic shape as with the tulip, but make them wider at the top.

Note: you may need to cut a slit half way down the sides and pinch them in for the first three petals (tape to hold).

There are more petals on a rosebud than a tulip so you will need to add two rows of three petals. The next three petals you need to make only need to reach the bottom of the nape of the bud. Tape these securely in place. The three outer ones, like the tulip will need to go right down to the base of the flower. Papier mache over all the petals, and while still damp, gently bend the tops to curve outwards to add realism. Leave to dry and add more layers to the petals.

"Ready for painting"

"Just like the real thing"

You can use this basic idea to create all kinds of flowers.

I painted this rosebud a beautiful peach colour to match these fresh roses that I was given.

Have
A DECO!

I was asked to make an umbrella stand in an art deco theme for a hallway. I decided to echo the square and angular shapes of the art deco period and so made a square stand with a staggered base. The "steps" I created by cutting out several pieces of corrugated cardboard in one inch varying widths.

Recycle a strong cardboard box

This project uses the basic layering method of papier mache.

From the cardboard, I measured and cut out all the pieces as shown. I coated the pieces with diluted pva glue to help prevent warping. When dry, I repeated on the reverse side.

Materials:

❖ 2 sheets of double corrugated cardboard
❖ Acrylic paint in soft green and gold
❖ Black enamel paint
❖ Polyurethane varnish

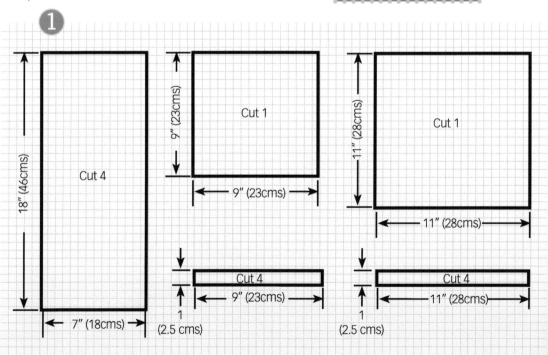

1

Cut 4 — 18" (46cms) × 7" (18cms)

Cut 1 — 9" (23cms) × 9" (23cms)

Cut 4 — 9" (23cms) × 1 (2.5 cms)

Cut 1 — 11" (28cms) × 11" (28cms)

Cut 4 — 11" (28cms) × 1 (2.5 cms)

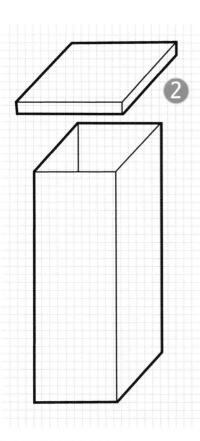

I took the four large rectangular pieces that will form the cylinder, and pasted layers of paper on one side. I repeated on the reverse side when dry.

Note: You may find it helpful to place large pieces like this under a heavy book when almost but not completely bone dry. This will help to make sure the sides remain perfectly flat.

I pasted again twice on both sides. When all the pieces were completely dry, I trimmed the edges. Using masking tape, I attached the pieces together and put them aside.

I took the two square pieces and stuck the four edging pieces to each base to form two plinths. I then covered the whole of these plinths with several layers of paper.

When all the pieces were completely dry, I measured one inch around the tops of the plinths with the black marker pen to act as a guide to help in the final assembly. I then placed the largest plinth on a flat table. Placing it directly on the black lines, I stuck the smaller plinth in the centre. Next, I placed the main body on top. All sections were securely taped together.

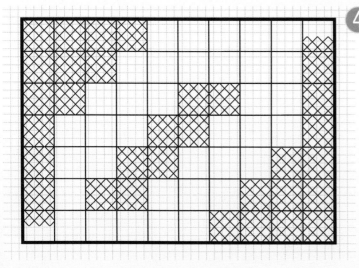

I marked a one-inch grid on a piece of the cardboard. Following the shaded patterns on the grid, I cut out the two "handles" and one decorative shape for the front. The handles were taped opposite sides of the stand, after measuring the centre point.

The decoration was glued to the front. I covered the handles and all the joins with more papier mache.

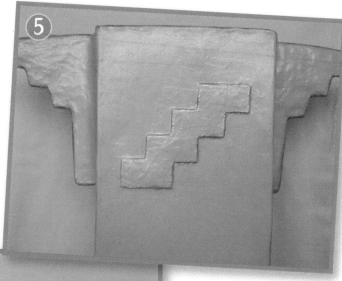

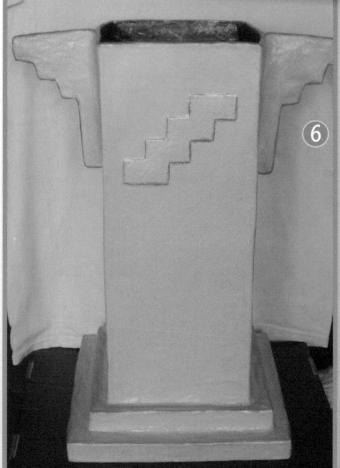

When it was dry, I lightly sanded it with fine sandpaper. Two coats of white emulsion paint were then applied.

The inside and the underneath was painted with black enamel paint. I thought this would give it a tougher surface. I painted the main body a light green and highlighted the edges with a light brushing of gold paint.

7

Finally, I varnished with clear polyurethane varnish. Three thin coats should be sufficient for a project like this, but it is best to sand lightly between the final coats.

Other options:
I have given you the measurements that I used so that you can get an idea of the scale. You will be able to work out your own set of measurements according to what you want to make. This stand could be made in a much smaller size as a pen/paintbrush holder for an arty desk. You could make a whole set of them in different sizes. The stand also makes an excellent container to show off large artificial flowers.

Chapter 7

Cheerful Clarice

Following on with the art deco theme, I decided to use Clarice Cliff as inspiration. Clarice made brightly coloured kitchen ware during this period, which became very popular, making her a household name.

You can imitate her style but use your own imagination so as not to plagiarise.

Clarice Cliff's works are now highly collectable today and very expensive. Now you can have your own brightly coloured pots for virtually no cost at all!

I made this pot using the layering method of papier mache. The pot is formed in exactly the same way as the tulips, the only difference was that I didn't paste quite so high up the sides of the balloon. When the pot was made and coated in emulsion paint I was ready to start the decoration. I studied pictures of Clarice Cliff's work and noted her style. Big blocks of bright colours, almost always outlined in black. If you want to do something similar, take a book out of the library with pictures of her work and make sketches to use as your guide.

Draw a rough plan of what you want to paint on the pot, varying the design to your own taste. Here is a drawing I did before painting my pot:

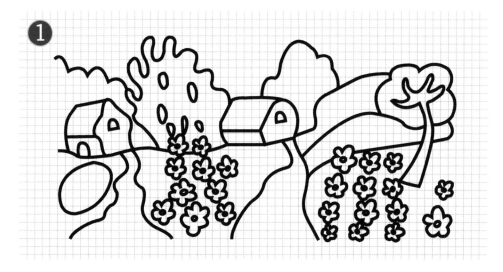

You could design any size or shape of pot, bowl and even plates. A large Clarice style plate would make a stunning decoration on a wall.

I took my adapted design right the way around the pot.

Chapter 8

Red October

As a spin-off from the art deco theme, I created this vase to capture the brilliant orange and red leaves that adorn the trees in autumn.

This is what I meant by one thing leading to another. Choosing a theme and then translating it into your own ideas is great fun and you still manage to create something unique.

This pot was made around a long cylindrical shaped balloon. These balloons are ideal for making vases.

It was covered in exactly the same way as the round balloons and I took it up to the height I wanted the vase to be.

A small circle of cardboard was cut for the base, just slightly bigger than the diameter of the vase. You can easily adjust this measurement according to the size of the balloon. The base was glued on and filled in with pasted scrunched newspaper in exactly the same way as the tulips.

The top was trimmed to make it level. I then cut two fin shaped pieces of cardboard for decoration either side of the base. These were attached with masking tape. A bit of care is needed in making sure that the two fins are equally spaced and vertical. They also need to be level with the top of the pot.

The fins were then covered in papier mache and left to dry.

Materials:

- ❖ Long straight balloon
- ❖ Cardboard
- ❖ Acrylic paint
- ❖ Polyurethane varnish

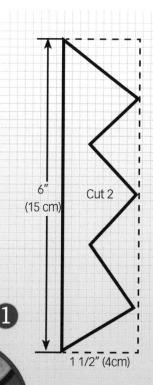

6" (15 cm)

Cut 2

1 1/2" (4cm)

❶

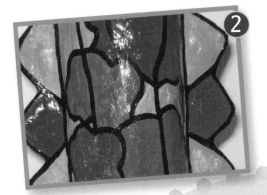

2 After the coating of white emulsion I penciled on a very simple tree design. I was still keeping to the Clarice Cliff theme of simple drawings in bold colours outlined in black.

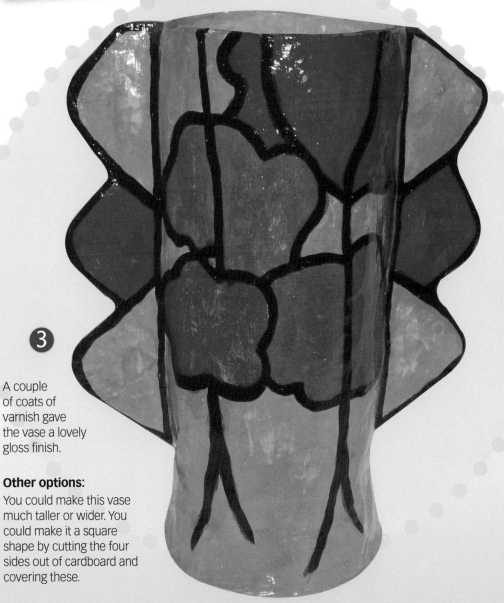

3

A couple of coats of varnish gave the vase a lovely gloss finish.

Other options:
You could make this vase much taller or wider. You could make it a square shape by cutting the four sides out of cardboard and covering these.

Pot POURRI Bowl

I wanted to make a pot pourri bowl and so I covered a balloon in the normal way, to give me the bowl shape. This time, though, I thought I would papier mache right up the sides of the balloon and use the rest of it to make a stand for my bowl.

When the required layers had been built up and had dried thoroughly, I cut my bowl shape out of the large rounded end. I looked at the remaining piece and thought about how I would use it for the stand.

I came up with the idea of cutting the covered balloon into several sections.

The bowl is decorated in coloured tissue paper and highlighted in gold acrylic paint. Filled with pot pourri and left to stand in an airy place, it will fill the room with fragrance. You could also fill the bowl with fruit as it would make a lovely centre piece on a dining table.

Materials:

- ❖ Small balloon
- ❖ Thin white card
- ❖ Coloured tissue paper - 3 shades of green, three shades of pink, purple
- ❖ Gold acrylic paint
- ❖ Sponge

Cover a balloon and dissect the pieces

I covered the whole balloon in strips of newspaper then left it to dry. I then repeated layering several times. When dry I burst the balloon and removed it. The neck edge was then trimmed level all round.

I cut the mould into three sections. Firstly, I marked 3 inches down from the neck edge. I drew a line right round and cut with a craft knife. This section was to form the stand. I measured and marked four equal curves and cut to form four legs.

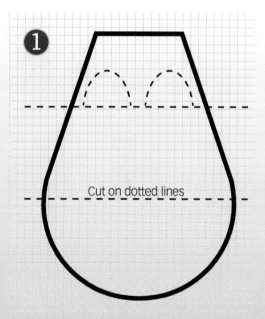

Cut on dotted lines

Next I measured 4 inches up from the base, cut and removed. This formed the bowl. The middle section was discarded from this project but was not thrown away. You can always keep any leftover shapes for another project! The bowl was placed on top of the stand and secured with masking tape. All joins were covered with more strips of paper, and also edges to give a smooth finish.

When it was completely dry it was painted with two coats of white emulsion paint. I cut 4 leaf shapes and 4 flower shapes from the thin white card using a craft knife.

The leaves were glued to the stand, and the flowers to the bowl.

Coloured tissue paper was torn into lots of small pieces ready to use. Diluted pva glue was brushed onto a small area of the bowl and I gently pressed on the tissue pieces, one at a time. Then I went on to the next area and continued covering the whole bowl until I had built up 2 or 3 layers. The pieces need to be overlapped over the other colours, it helps them to blend into one another.

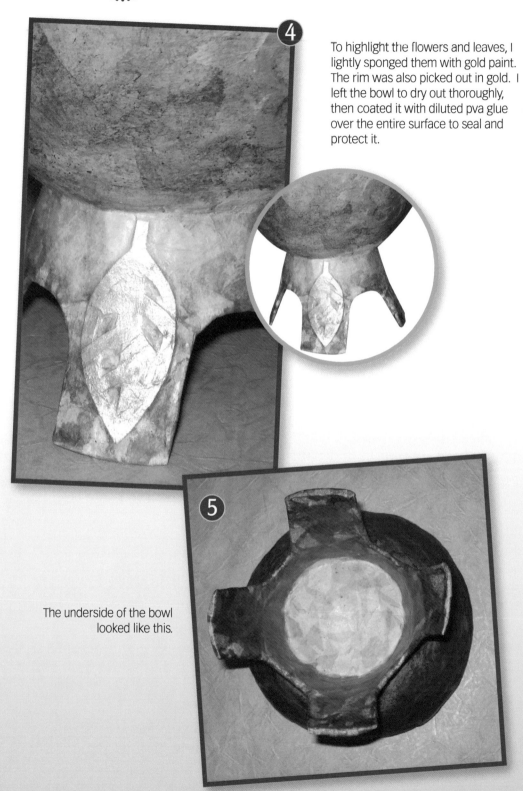

4 To highlight the flowers and leaves, I lightly sponged them with gold paint. The rim was also picked out in gold. I left the bowl to dry out thoroughly, then coated it with diluted pva glue over the entire surface to seal and protect it.

5

The underside of the bowl looked like this.

6

Other options.

You can easily adapt this idea to many other forms. You could use a much bigger balloon or a long thin one. You could even mix cut parts from both and mix them to get some original shapes. One idea is to cover several different size and shaped balloons and when they are thoroughly dry you can study them. All sorts of ideas will come into your head as you look at the shapes. Cut some in half diagonally and some horizontally. Turn them upside down and hold different shapes together. Let your imagination run riot.

Chapter 10

Tray It With Love

I was asked to make a heart shaped tray for Valentine's Day. I thought of the usual heart shapes and wanted to do something a little different.

You see a lot of heart shaped balloons around and I got the idea to make a heart shaped balloon style tray - with a slight twist!

The tray was simple to make and with its floating heart-shaped balloon design in bright colours, it made it a little out of the ordinary.

Put your heart into it

On a large sheet of heavy corrugated cardboard, I marked a 1 inch grid. I then carefully drew on the heart shape using the guide.

Materials:
- ❖ Double corrugated cardboard
- ❖ Sheet of paper
- ❖ Scissors
- ❖ Ruler
- ❖ Marker pen
- ❖ White (pva) glue
- ❖ Newspaper
- ❖ Wallpaper paste
- ❖ White emulsion paint
- ❖ Sandpaper
- ❖ Acrylic paint
- ❖ Polyurethane varnish

I cut out the shape. Next I cut a 1 inch strip by 49 inches approx' of the same cardboard.

Tip: You can use several short lengths provided that you join them together end to end carefully with masking tape.

To get the narrow cardboard strip to bend nicely around the heart shape, I scored it with a pair of scissors across the width at regular intervals. Placing the heart shape on a table, I gently eased the strip to follow the heart shape and sit nicely on top of the outer edges. I then secured it in place with glue and masking tape. Using diluted pva (white glue), the entire tray was sealed to prevent warping.

The top of the tray was then covered with its first layer of papier mache. When dry, the reverse was pasted. This was repeated several times until the whole tray had 6 or 7 layers. (It was left to dry in between layers). When it was completely dry, I painted it with two coats of white emulsion.

On a sheet of paper I drew a small grid and marked out heart shapes in three different sizes, then cut them out. Using these shapes as templates, I placed them on the tray and marked all around them with a marker pen. Some were overlapped, but I made sure that some of them remained a whole heart shape. I took the patterns right up to the rim, and gently folded the edges over the lip of the tray to take the colour over the top.

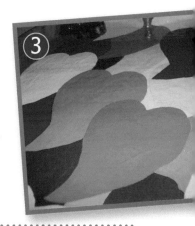

The hearts can be painted in as many different colours as you like. I wanted a brightly coloured tray. Finally, I varnished with a polyurethane gloss varnish (two coats), then very lightly rubbed it down with sandpaper before applying a third coat.

Optional:

You may prefer to use coloured paper for the shapes and/or stick to more traditional colours.

January BLUES

Blue is often thought of as a cold colour, but it is also very soothing, fresh and lively - the ideal colour to put you in the mood for new beginnings. I wanted to make a large decorative bowl that would look nice as a centerpiece on a table.

Peaceful, tranquil blue – the colour of the sky and the ocean

A large balloon was blown up and knotted tightly. I then covered it with a layer of pasted strips of newspaper. I left it to dry and repeated. About 7 layers were gradually built up.

I burst the balloon and removed it from the inside. I measured and cut out a large circle of cardboard to make the base. You need to cut the cardboard circle to the size of your balloon, and take into consideration how big you want the base to be.

I put a blob of glue in the centre of the cardboard and placed the base of the mould on top of it. It was secured in place with several large pasted pieces of paper, scrunched up, then left to dry.

More scrunched layers of newspaper were added until the base had formed a nice natural looking curve. The whole area was then covered with more paper strips until it was completely smooth. When dry it was painted white.

I drew swirls all around the pot, of varying heights, then carefully cut them out with scissors.

Materials:
- ❖ 2 large balloons
- ❖ Cardboard
- ❖ Marker Pen
- ❖ Sharp scissors
- ❖ Newspaper
- ❖ White paper
- ❖ Wallpaper paste
- ❖ Glue
- ❖ Sandpaper
- ❖ Acrylic paint
- ❖ Small round sponge
- ❖ Glass nuggets

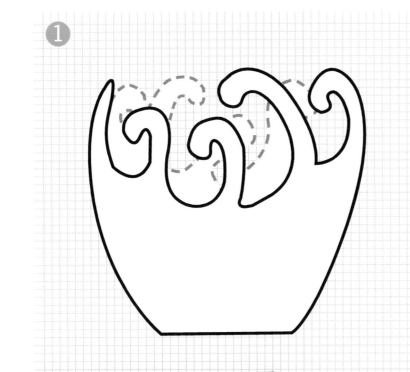

The whole pot was covered again with more paper strips, with particular attention paid to the necks of the swirls. When finished, I placed another balloon of the same size into the pot and blew it up to firmly, but not tightly press against the sides of the swirls. I did this to ensure that all the swirls dried in the correct shape.

When dry, I burst and removed the balloon and covered with one layer of white paper strips. When completely dry, I painted the whole of the inside a light colour. Metallic paint was painted onto the outside. Two coats are generally required. To decorate the inside, I dipped a round shaped sponge lightly into two different shades of blue and sponged them randomly over the surface. Finally, I gave it highlights by sponging on circles in silver.

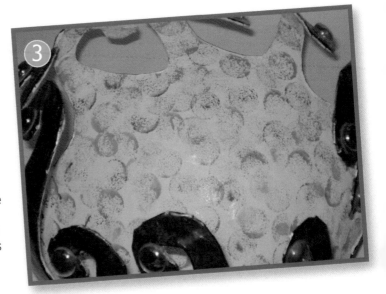

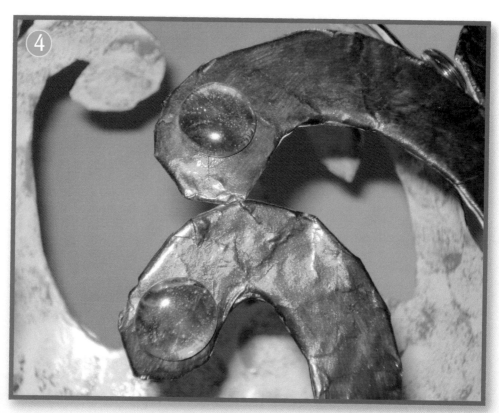

Glass nuggets were glued to the tip of each swirl.

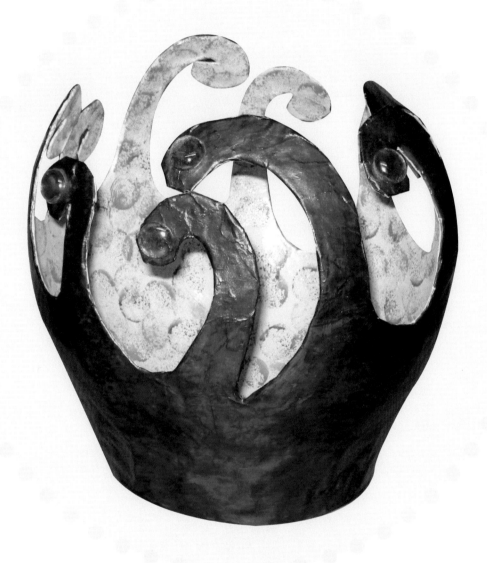

⑤

Other Ideas: You can use any other colour combinations to suit any room theme.

This ornamental pot can be filled with polished stones, glass nuggets or pot pourri or just used on its own for a designer effect. You could make it very small or very large.

TUTANKHA-MEN'S *Gifts*

Men are always very difficult to get presents for and I wanted to make something practical as well as original.

I have a love of Egyptian things and chose this theme to base my gift on. I looked through my books on ancient Egypt and my attention was drawn to a picture taken inside Tutankhamen's tomb. I loved the decorative panel at the back of the room, and the impressive dogs of Anubis guarding the treasures. I wanted to capture these images into one piece of work, but make something useful at the same time.

I chose a letter rack. I thought the panel at the back of the tomb would make a lovely backing for my rack, and a dog of Anubis could sit either side and guard the important letters!

These pictures were taken from "Time Life Books" "Lost Civilizations, Egypt: Land Of The Pharaohs."

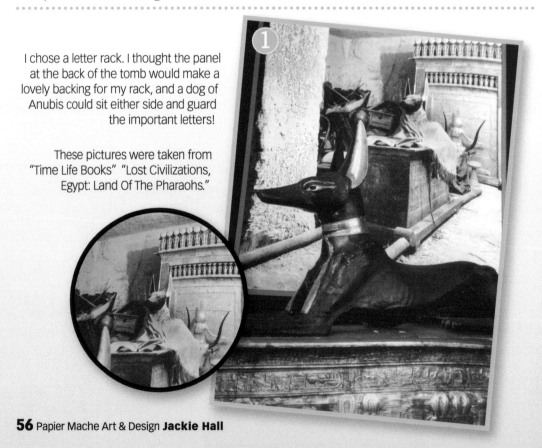

Egypt's treasures from a cardboard box

I measured and marked out all the pieces onto a piece of strong cardboard. I have given the sizes I used here to give you a guide, but you can make it longer, taller or wider to your choice. You could have a lot more dividing sections and make some of varying widths. The base is 10 inches long by 6 inches wide. The back is 7 ½ inches high and the front 3 inches high.

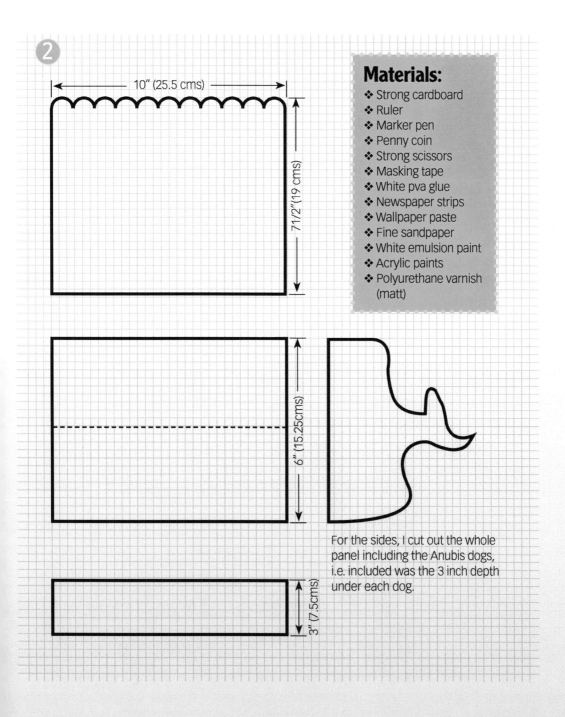

Materials:
- ❖ Strong cardboard
- ❖ Ruler
- ❖ Marker pen
- ❖ Penny coin
- ❖ Strong scissors
- ❖ Masking tape
- ❖ White pva glue
- ❖ Newspaper strips
- ❖ Wallpaper paste
- ❖ Fine sandpaper
- ❖ White emulsion paint
- ❖ Acrylic paints
- ❖ Polyurethane varnish (matt)

10" (25.5 cms)

7 1/2" (19 cms)

6" (15.25cms)

3" (7.5cms)

For the sides, I cut out the whole panel including the Anubis dogs, i.e. included was the 3 inch depth under each dog.

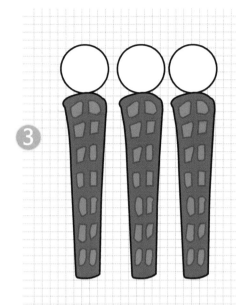

For the back panel, I measured across the top and divided it into ten equal sections. A penny coin was very useful to draw around.

When all the pieces had been cut out, I placed the base flat down on the table. I measured and marked out the centre and drew a line right across it. This gave me the right position to fix the dividing shelf. The back was attached using masking tape. Next the sides and front were taped in place. Finally, using my marked line across the middle, I taped the divider in place.

I now had a sturdy shell. I brushed the whole piece with diluted pva glue (you don't want any warping on a precision item like this).

The building up of my papier mache strips followed, allowing plenty of time to dry in between layers. For the dogs, I used very small pieces of pasted paper, so as not to make them too thick. I also wanted them to look smooth and sleek. I built up a bit more texture around the middle of the dog's heads to give them more of a 3D look.

When completely dry, I lightly rubbed with fine sandpaper to give a smooth finish. This is particularly important on the dogs. Then the whole letter rack was painted with white emulsion.

With a pencil, I drew the patterns on the back, and the dogs' features. Then comes the fun part of painting in all the details. As a guide, I have used the following colours: For the inside of the letter rack I have used a sandy colour. The back is a blue and red pattern on a black background, with white discs at the top. The dogs are black with gold features. The front and sides are gold. To paint the hieroglyphics on the sides, I mixed some gold paint with a little burnt sienna.

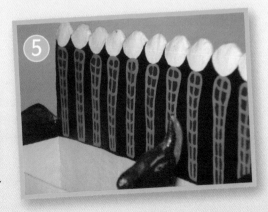

6

Finally, it was protected with a couple of coats of matt polyurethane varnish.

LARGE PROJECTS

with

Armatures

When making a very large item with papier mache, you will need to make an armature and you basically have two choices in how to do this.

Firstly, you could build up your project using boxes, slabs of polystyrene or anything else that you find lying around (provided it is fairly light). There are fors and against for this method. You will have the chance to build it up gradually, and it is fairly quick to do, but you will have to join everything up carefully so as not to have boxy shapes sticking out through your papier mache.

The other way is to make a framework out of wire netting. The advantage of this is that you can make it to the exact shape that you require. It takes much longer to build, but it is very much quicker to cover in papier mache and get an even surface. The downside is the handling of the wire. You will need to wear protective gloves when cutting the netting as it has very sharp ends.

The best way to build an armature out of netting is to have a good think first about the size you want the final project to be. In the case of my life-sized dog, the size was determined for me. With my elephant, I wanted to make it as big as I possibly could – and still get it out through my front door!

You need small sectioned wire netting, some thick fencing wire (to hold the netting in place) and it is really helpful to have some thin wire too. This you can cut into small pieces and literally use it to "stitch" the netting onto the wire.

Make a rough shape out of the strong wire, and then cut pieces of wire netting to cover it. Use the thin wire to fix it in place every few inches. Make sure that you twist the ends of the wire thoroughly, and that the ends lie inside the project.

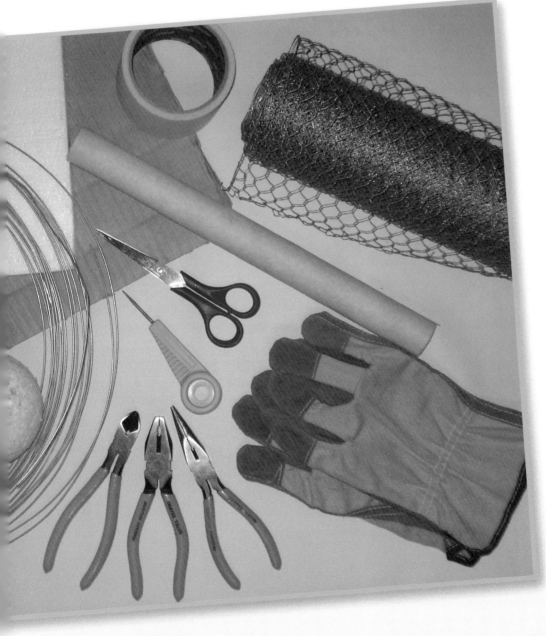

Life-sized Basset hound

Owning a Basset hound, I had my model there to help me. With the elephant I was not so fortunate, so I had to research many books. It is surprising how little you find you actually know about something when you come to draw a picture or make something. For instance, how many people know how far up the side of the face the eyes are, or where exactly the tusks come out. Spending time now saves much wasted time later on altering things.

Start with a very basic wire shape. It won't look much like whatever it is you are hoping to make at this stage, but it will soon will.

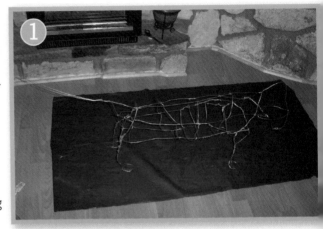

Next comes the building out of the shape with wire netting. You will need wire cutters for this job. Bend and twist the pieces before adding them to the wire frame. When they are in place, you can still manoeuvre them about.

Masking tape is very useful to wrap round the wire frame. It not only helps to hold the whole thing together, it also gives something for the papier mache to attach itself to.

Cover with papier mache in the usual way

I have painted the basset white as although I had decided to use coloured paper rather than painting, I wanted to get the design right by drawing on the dog's patterns.

I was making it for someone who had two bassets and they wanted a papier mache dog to represent both of them.

6

When you are trying to get a likeness of a pet, it is helpful to watch the animal and note its peculiarities. It might have a particular way of holding its head, walking or sitting. If you can bring one of these elements into your work, it will add greatly to the realism and make the animal instantly recognisable.

Here is the finished Basset.
The coat is completely coloured
paper. The head is taken from
one of the dogs.

7

The body is taken
from the other one.

Elephant

As I was asked to make this elephant for a specific purpose, I did a rough sketch first. I thought it was to be for all recycling, but then was told it was for just paper.

I then made a model out of plasticine. This is a really useful medium to use. When you have made the model, you can turn it round and view it from all sides, including the top. You can play around with the model until you are completely happy about its proportions.

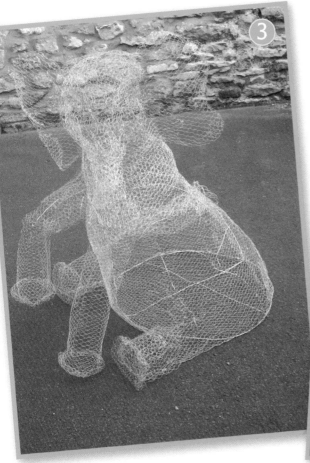

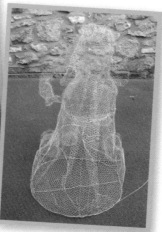

I started off my elephant with a circle of thick wire and checked to see if it would indeed fit through my doorway. Once I was happy that I wouldn't have to take the door frame off to move it, I placed this circle of wire on the floor and started to turn it into an elephant! A daunting prospect at this stage, but you soon learn that mighty oaks from acorns do grow!

I made the wire netting frame as I had with the dog. You will be able to see the thick wire running through it. The elephant itself is completely hollow.

Some masking tape "bandaging" and you are ready to papier mache. The beauty of using a hollow wire frame is that the papier mache will dry quite quickly, as air is able to get to both sides of it. You will only be able to paste one side at a time, turning it over to do the other side when dry.

To get the crinkly look to his trunk, I pasted large pieces of newspaper and lay these on the surface. I then gently slid the paper into creases. This is a case where wallpaper paste is such an excellent adhesive as you can slip and slide your paper into position without it suddenly going dry and hard.

5 I wanted a natural looking elephant, not a comical cartoon character, but I wanted it to look friendly and approachable so that it would appeal to children, so I gave it slightly larger eyes than an elephant would have.

And a large open mouth with just a hint of a smile!

I used pink pieces of paper torn out of magazines for the mouth, and light brown paper for his toenails.

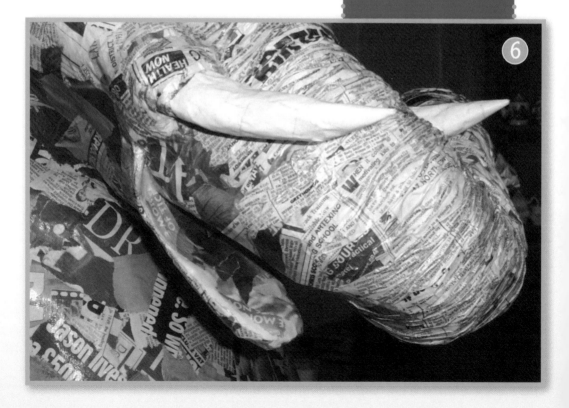

6

7

A few coats of diluted pva glue gave him a bit of
protection, then he left home to start his new life!

Chapter 14

Klimt Clock

The well known artist Klimt was the inspiration behind this clock. I just love the patterns he painted and the copious amounts of gold he used.

I decided on this curvy shape as I have a mirror in a similar pattern and I wanted it to look in keeping on my wall.

I cut a baseboard in double corrugated cardboard and sealed it with diluted pva glue. I covered it both sides with several layers of papier mache that had dried in between.

I wanted a rough texture for the surface of my clock so I added a layer of pulped papier mache to the top side. This was smoothed down and left to dry thoroughly.

When dry, I painted it white so that I could draw my design on.

Picture taken from
"Pocket Art Klimt"
Published by Grange Books.

I bought a clock movement for the back. These are usually very inexpensive. It was a square shape, so I carved out a square indent for the clock to sit in. By using double corrugated cardboard, it meant that I only needed to go through half of the thickness. I then drilled a hole through the centre for the hands to go through. Using Klimt's work to guide me, I designed my very own Klimt style clock. I drew lots of small designs as he did, and used plenty of gold. When I had finished painting I sealed it with varnish.

To fix the clock in place, the hands need to be carefully removed. The clock is then glued into place at the back. The hands are then gently pressed back into place from the front.

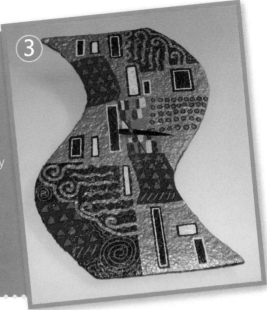

You could use any shape you like to make a clock, and any artist to use for inspiration. Placing it on a brightly coloured wall really brings out the lively colours in the clock.

Passion Flower Pot

A lot of people have asked me how I made the passion flower on this pot. Some flowers are easier to do than others, and I have to say the passion flower is quite complex. I was inspired to make this pot as I have a passion flower growing all around my front door. I adore the flowers and the twirly tendrils often get caught in my hair when I walk in and out of the door.

I love big pots and I wanted to recreate the vine-like passion flower climbing and twining around one just like it does around my archway.

I took several pictures of the flower and observed it from different angles. The sepals are quite high on the flower and the middle is very detailed.

The leaves are hand-like in shape.

(2)

To create a plant like the passion flower you are going to need wire as I used. The stems are too narrow for anything else to make a strong enough stalk.

Lots of paper strips wound round the wire stems will make the right thickness. The main stem will be the thickest (with the most layers of paper), tapering out to the ends. I made my climbing plant with the exception of the flower itself and the tendils, then fixed it to the sides of the pot. The bottom of the wire I poked through a hole I made near the base. This stopped any ends being on show and made it safer. I twisted the stems around the pot in as natural looking way as I could then taped them fully in place with masking tape.

(3)

I wanted this project to look subtle so I decided to use coloured tissue paper to decorate it rather than paint. On the leaves I used several different shades of green tissue which has given it a nice graded look. The raised letters I made very simply from pieces of pasted newspaper twisted to form the letters, then covered them in silver tissue.

④ The flower I built up afterwards using card covered in papier mache for the petals. There were several thin wires running through the centre. These were then gently twisted out to form the intricate shapes in the middle.

I used paint on the flower itself due to the "fringe" around the edge which would have been impossible to cover with tissue.

⑤

The tendrils on the passion flower plant resemble corkscrews. These I made from thin wire pasted with green tissue.

6

I used diluted pva glue to paste the tissue on so I sealed it with the same medium. It gave it a nice soft sheen which suited the tissue.

Fern Crozier

I have a love of tropical plants and have several tree ferns from New Zealand in my garden. I find watching the tight little curls of the new fronds intensely interesting. They spring up out of the centre of the trunk in a similar way to ordinary ferns, but these are so spectacular by their sheer size. I just felt I had to create one of these croziers in papier mache.

I started off with a long piece of stiff wire. I fixed it to a square base consisting of two pieces of double corrugated cardboard stuck together. The base of the wire was pushed through the base of the cardboard (you can use an awl to do this) and secured top and bottom with masking tape and wedges of pasted paper.

①

Wire armature on base

I looked around to find something suitable to make the fleshy parts of the crozier. I needed something smooth and of an even thickness. I saw some pipe insulation on an outside tap and thought this was ideal. It is spongy and soft, very lightweight and affordable.

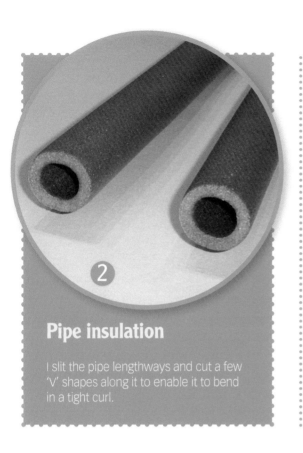

Pipe insulation

I slit the pipe lengthways and cut a few 'V' shapes along it to enable it to bend in a tight curl.

Cut-outs to allow for tight bending

I slipped the tubing around the wire armature and secured it with masking tape. I found it helpful to cover the majority of the piping with masking tape to give the papier mache something to hold on to.

Attaching tube to wire frame

It was then on to the papier mache. Small pieces of pasted paper were gently pushed into the grooves. Then the layers of papier mache added. The base had several layers too, and just before I'd finished, I added some tiny whispy bits that appear on these ferns, made from pieces of pasted newspaper folded and bent into shape. They were then glued onto the dried surface. The joins of these were then secured with a few more strips of paper.

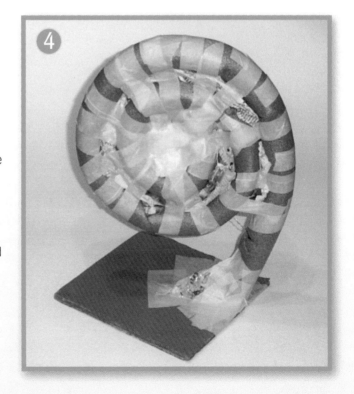

Adding the details and papier mache

After coating it with two coats of white emulsion, I noticed a couple of places that needed to be built up a little more.

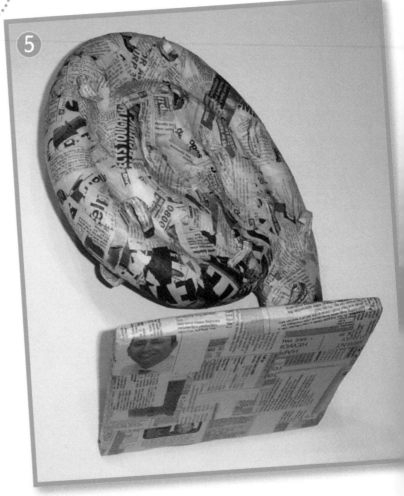

White coating

Finally the really fun part – the painting! I mixed several shades of green acrylic paint to get the look I was wanting. Small smudges of the different greens were added to give colour contrasts and shading effects by dry brushing very dark green into the grooves and yellow onto the raised surfaces.

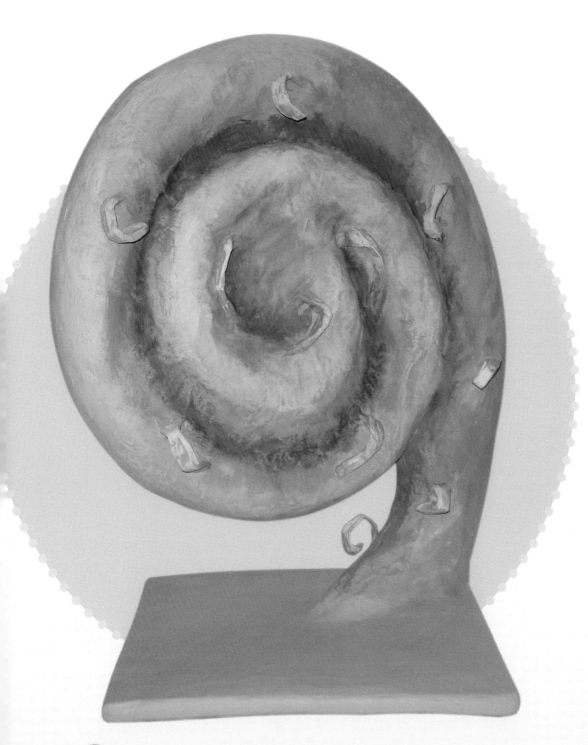

7 Now I am able to admire these stunning plants all year round.

Other IDEAS

These pots are made in exactly the same way as all the other pots in that they are formed round a balloon and have a base added.

Head in the clouds

This pot was cut down quite low and has a wide flat rim. To make a rim like this cut the bowl all around to the same height. Place it upside down onto a piece of corrugated cardboard. Draw round the pot with a marker pen. Decide how wide you want the rim to be and measure out an outer ring.

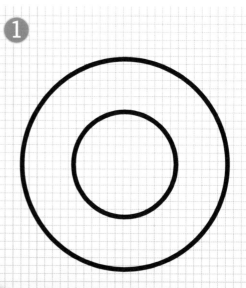

1

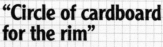

"Circle of cardboard for the rim"

2

Attach this ring to the top of the bowl and secure with masking tape. Cover the rim with papier mache, taking the strips right down the side of the pot and into the inside.

I wanted to make a dramatic looking pot so I chose bold coloured cloud patterns outlined in black

③ Cloud patterns

④

A couple of coats of gloss varnish was all that was needed to complete the look.

Rough with the smooth

An interesting surface can be achieved by using two starkly contrasting finishes. This pot has been left with very high sides and I have added two handles. To make handles like this, cut two pieces of cardboard as shown.

The handles were attached with masking tape and covered with papier mache. When thoroughly dry, I made the very bumpy surface by taking hold of strips of pasted newspaper and twisting them. I then laid them horizontally around the pot. You only need to add one layer of these twisted strips if you want to have a uniform result. Gently push each piece close to the one that has just been laid, as if you were weaving a rug. The handles are covered in exactly the same way.

②

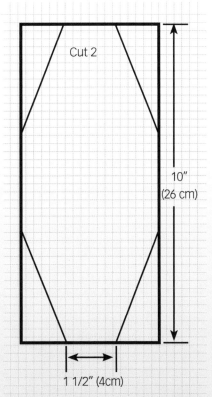

①

Cut 2

10"
(26 cm)

1 1/2" (4cm)

"Cut two for pot handles"

③

Before you get too carried away and cover the whole pot, stop and leave an area uncovered. I have left the base area, but you could have a smooth top or a smooth patch in the middle.

④

To give impact, the smooth area needs to be super smooth. I did this by rubbing lightly with sandpaper and smearing over a little household filler. The pot then had the emulsion coat of paint.

Painting a pot like this is very interesting. I've used a multitude of colours for mine, but you could choose just one or two colours.

Give us a twirl

This pot has an "open shirt" design for the neck. You don't have to stick to level openings! All you need to do to create this look is to cut down from the back of the pot, sloping towards the front, taking care to get each side matching. Bring both sides down to a point, however low you want the neckline to be.

Measure the total distance around the opening (you will find it easier to use a piece of string for this). Cut a strip of thin cardboard to the length of the piece of string. Decide how high you want the back of the collar to be and make this the width of the piece of cardboard. Draw lines sloping down from the middle each side. I have done mine parallel, but you could do an unbalanced pattern if you preferred.

Attach the collar to the pot with masking tape. If it is not quite a perfect fit, you can snip little bits away with a pair of scissors. It won't notice when it is covered with papier mache! While you are adding the pasted strips of paper, the card will absorb some of the moisture. You now have a golden opportunity to gently bend and twist the collar into the shape you are after. You can even give it a fluted look as I have done.

I thought the shape lent itself to some flamboyant colours so I painted the inside (you can really show off the inside with a neckline like this) a shocking pink. I painted the outside a metallic purple with bright yellow swirls.

4

As I was painting the outside design on the pot, I felt I had seen that pattern somewhere before, but I couldn't think where. Then someone called on me then rushed out. They came back shortly afterwards with a bar of chocolate! I must have had chocolate on my mind. Advertisers don't choose bold designs for nothing! At least I then knew where I'd got the inspiration from!

Moss pot

For this pot I wanted to make a raised pattern representing rock pools and moss. I did this by using pasted strips of newspaper and draping them in loops around the pot. I then put more papier mache over the whole pot, smoothing it down over the loops. When dry I painted it white so that I could see my design much more clearly.

This pot was really fun to paint. I went to town with different shades of green, with splashes of yellow, blue and red. I painted the loops silver. I wanted the pot to really shine and shimmer, so I dabbed some metallic green and yellow paint with a natural sponge after the other paint had dried.

The back of the pot is not covered in loops, so I dry brushed some red and purple paint to resemble flowers.

To give extra sparkle, I glued some tiny caviar beads in the centre of each loop. To do this, simply paste some glue where you want the beads to stick and shake the beads on top of it. When dry, shake off the excess beads. If you are careful to only put the glue exactly where you want the beads to be, you can achieve a very natural look, appearing that the beads have fallen into the loops and stayed there on their own accord.

Barrel of Laughs

Just as you can make a pot from a large balloon, you can also make a barrel shape! The top needs to be cut down much further than you would do for a pot, and the base, made up in a similar way to the tulips and pots, has to be very much wider.

I decided to use coloured paper for this project, and to make life easier I used brown paper (to represent wood) on my very first covering of the balloon. This is a very good way to cover the inside of a pot, bowl or barrel. As you can see in the photo, the inside of the barrel is already papered, leaving just the outside to cover.

The Barrel

You will need to cut two circles the same diameter from double corrugated cardboard. One will form the base, the other a lid.

3 The double corrugated cardboard base will take more filling in round the sides with scrunched up pasted newspaper, taking longer to dry than for pots.

4

I got round the long drying problem by pricking some holes in the base of the cardboard with an awl. This helped to let air into the inside of the barrel and it consequently dried more quickly. Doing this won't cause any damage to the structure, and further layers of papier mache will hide the holes. You can do this trick with some of the smaller pots if you think they will take too long to dry out.

5

The whole barrel was completely covered in strips of the same brown paper, including both sides of the lid.

6 Using some grey coloured paper, I made "metal" trims to go round the barrel. I put several layers on to give the strips a bit of depth.

The laughing man

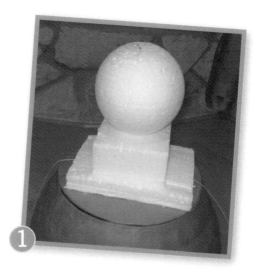

To make the head and shoulders, I used some rectangular pieces of polystyrene that had been used for protection for an electrical item I bought. I used pva glue to stick two pieces of the same size onto the top of the barrel lid. When the glue had dried, I glued a smaller, wider chunk in the middle for the neck.

For the head I used a polystyrene ball that had once been covered in tiny mirrors. I had pinched all the mirrors from it and used them to decorate other projects!

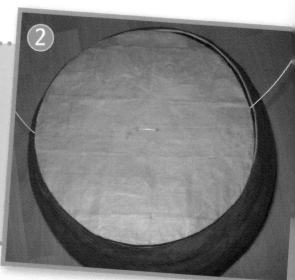

To secure the whole lot together and fix on the head, I got a long piece of tough wire and bending it in half, pushed it through from the underside of the lid. Though the head would be perfectly fine without the wire once it was covered in papier mache and dried. However, if you have ever tried to papier mache something which is wobbling about, you will understand why I used the wire!

③

A long cardboard tube was ideal to make the arms. I cut the tube in half and slid one half on the wire either side. To give the head and shoulders a bit more shape, I used a small hand saw to trim off the sharp corners. Masking tape can be used to wrap round parts that you need to tighten up. I wound some all the way down the arms and used it to form fingers.

To make a pulp out of paper, you just need to tear the paper up into small pieces and boil in a saucepan of water for about ½ an hour.

④

⑤

I wanted to make a laughing man but didn't want it to look conventional. Don't ask me why, but I wanted to make a yellow man! He needed to be a cartoon type character with exaggerated features.
I got together lots of sheets of yellow paper. Some of it was a light yellow and some had a more orange tone.

The use of a liquidizer is a real boon when making pulp, especially with thick paper. You can use virtually anything to beat the paper pieces down, including stirring it, rubbing the pieces together between your fingers or whisking it. By far the easiest though is to use a liquidizer. There is no need to buy an expensive one. You can usually find second hand ones going fairly cheap. You won't want to use it for food afterwards so it will need to be stored with your other kitchen salvaged items!

Whatever method you use, it is a painstaking process making pulp. If you liquidize, you must put 4 or 5 times more water in than paper, otherwise it will jam up the blades at the bottom. To say how long it will take to break down your paper is impossible to predict, as there are so many different types and thicknesses of paper.

In my batch of yellow pulp where I used a mixture of papers, some pieces broke down more quickly than others. You will know when it is reduced to a pulp just by looking at it.

A large sieve is useful to drain the pulp. Take a good handful at a time and squeeze most of the remaining water out. Finally add your wallpaper paste and pva and you are away!

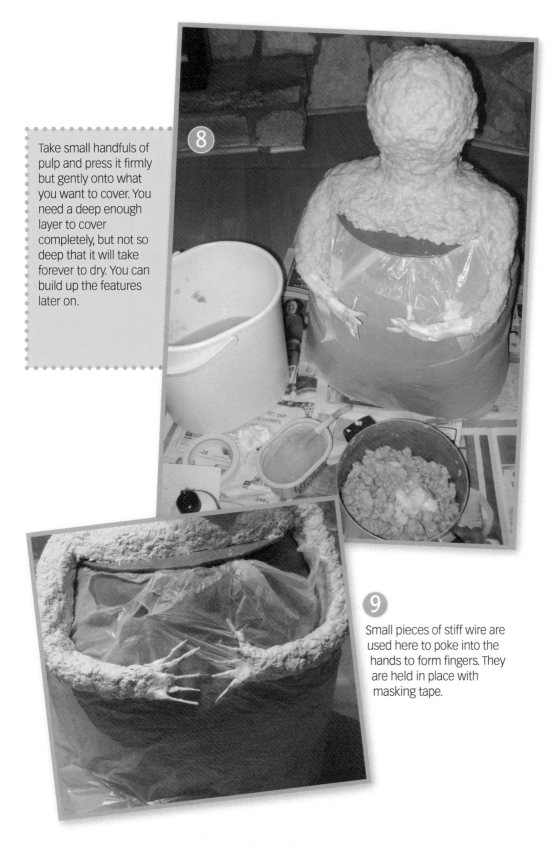

Take small handfuls of pulp and press it firmly but gently onto what you want to cover. You need a deep enough layer to cover completely, but not so deep that it will take forever to dry. You can build up the features later on.

⑧

⑨

Small pieces of stiff wire are used here to poke into the hands to form fingers. They are held in place with masking tape.

⑩

Another good layer of paper pulp over the whole body as well as the fingers and he starts to resemble a little person. It is wise to leave the smaller details until you have built up the face and body, otherwise they may shrink and disappear in the drying. When you have a really dry body, it should be rock hard. You can then build up tiny amounts as I have done here to give the impression that his eyes are screwed up with laughing so much.

The teeth are made from white toilet paper. This gave him a lovely set of pearly whites. To make the pulp, use the same technique as for skin in "The Arty Bit".

The tongue is made in the same way – this time using red tissue paper. (I've never seen bright red toilet paper!) Tissue paper is a bit more resistant to pulping surprisingly, but you get there in the end.

The only paint I used was a thin line to highlight the eye creases.

I coated him in diluted pva glue to seal the pulp and give it a bit of protection.

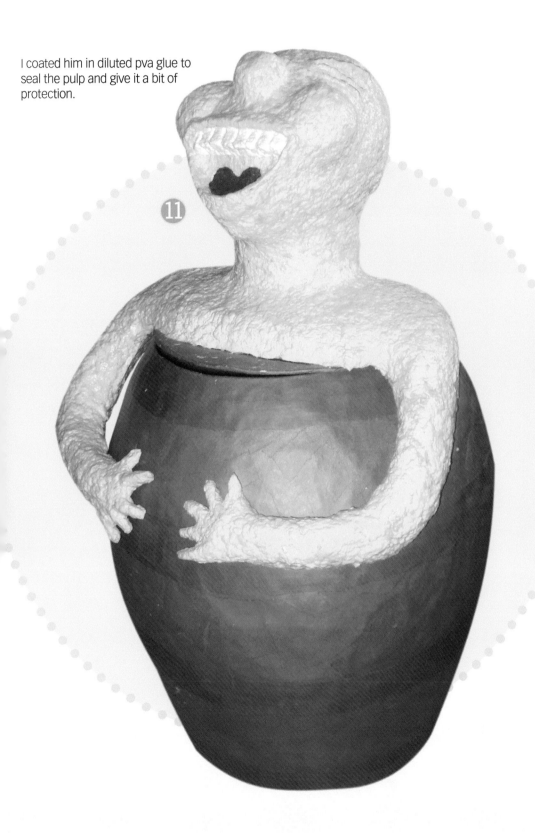

Pride & Prejudice

I wanted to challenge myself to see if I could make a diorama in 100% papier mache. My aim was to have everything that was visible to the eye to be paper, with no hint of plaster, filler or gesso.

As a fan of Pride and Prejudice, it didn't take me long to come up with a subject matter! This model of Elizabeth and Darcy shows just what can be made using entirely recycled objects and paper. I made an armature from items lying around my house – cardboard, polystyrene, thin card and scraps of wire. Everything you can actually see on the surface is made of one type of paper or another.

Follow me on my journey

Firstly I decided what size I wanted the two figures to be. I didn't want them too small and not too large either so I settled on around 15". I looked around for pictures of Elizabeth and Darcy from the recent BBC adaption. I not only liked the televised version very much but I thought it would be more of a challenge to base the figures on real life characters rather than fictitious drawings. I scoured magazines and newspapers and collected many pictures of them taken from all angles. It was very important to me to get the figures accurate from all sides, as this project, like all 3D work, is meant to be viewed from several angles.

Materials:
- ❖ Double corrugated cardboard
- ❖ Single corrugated cardboard
- ❖ Thin cardboard
- ❖ Polystyrene
- ❖ Masking tape
- ❖ White (pva) glue
- ❖ Wallpaper paste
- ❖ Paper towel roll holders
- ❖ Jewellery findings
- ❖ Metallic braid
- ❖ Satin polyurethane varnish
- ❖ Newspaper
- ❖ Tissue paper

I thought about what pose I wanted them in, and felt that two standing figures would be the most suited to what I wanted to achieve. I then had to decide what backdrop I wanted. I went for a fireplace with a large mirror above as this would reflect the back of their heads and allow the figures to be viewed from the back.

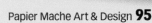

ARMATURE

The base and backing board

I cut up a large cardboard box (double corrugated) and cut two rectangular pieces for the base. I glued the two pieces together with pva glue for extra strength. To give ample room both at the sides and front of the figures, but still keeping it on the narrow side, I cut the pieces 8 ½" by 16 ½".

I then cut one piece of the same thickness cardboard for the backing. It was the same width as the longest length of the rectangular pieces and 23" high. I cut the backing in a wavy fashion to give a representation of the wall behind and to let the imagination believe that the wall and mirror went on passed the scene.

The backing piece I then put aside. This was to be added much later on as I needed to be able to work on the back of the two figures, whose heads would protrude a little over the top of the fireplace.

The fireplace

I did a bit of research into the style and height of Regency fireplaces and found a piece of polystyrene that was just right for a fireplace. It was a piece of end packaging from an electrical item and was the thickness I required (1 ½") It was hollow so was perfect for the three sides I needed. If you are not lucky enough to find the right size piece, you can very easily make it from small off-cuts of polystyrene, glued with white glue and taped together with masking tape. I now had the basic fireplace shape. The next thing to do was to build up the top and sides to give it authenticity. The fire surrounds of this period were very grand, with panelling and often having marble columns at the sides. I built up the jutting sides at the top with pieces of thin cardboard wrapped around small chunks of polystyrene and glued these to the main frame. I used pva and taped them for extra strength.

The figures

Having decided what height I wanted the figures, I cut some fencing wire and bent it into a very crude figure of a man. Darcy was the tallest figure so I started on him and made him 15" high. I used one long piece of wire for the main body, folded in half with a loop at the top for the head. A larger loop for the body, twisting the two wires together to hold both loops. The two wires were then splayed out to form the legs. I positioned these in the stance I wanted him in (standing up with a straight back, but with one knee slightly bent and foot turning outwards). A shorter piece of wire was used for the arms twisted into the main body frame. One of his hands was to be clasped in front of him, and the other arm straight down by his side.

Elizabeth was made in exactly the same way, proportionally shorter than Darcy. I wanted her to have her head slightly tilted so that she was looking across and slightly up at Darcy. Her hands were to be stretched out in front of her.

At this stage the whole thing looks incredibly crude, and it is hard to imagine them ever looking like real people. Perseverance really does pay off, and it is worth spending a good deal of time fiddling about with the wire armatures until you are happy with the proportions and pose. You can of course alter them slightly a little later on, that being the benefit of using wire, but you don't want to be making drastic alterations too far down the line or it will throw everything out.

This completed the first stage of my diorama. The armature is a very important part, not only to give you something to build your work onto, but to give it strength and durability.

Putting the framework together

The first thing I did (and a very important tip) was to brush some diluted pva glue onto all the exposed cardboard surfaces. Two coats is a good idea. This will help to seal the cardboard and make it less likely to warp when you add the wet paper.

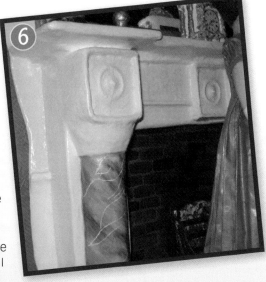

Still leaving the backing board aside (I would not be adding that for some time), I positioned and glued the polystyrene fireplace onto the base. I glued it in the centre of the back, just in a bit to allow for the backing board to be added later. Your own measurements will vary so just check the width and make allowances for this. I used strips of masking tape as well as glue to hold it in place, taking the tape right under the base for good measure.

I cut two small rectangular pieces of thick cardboard to form the bases of the two columns and glued these both to the fireplace and floor. The "marble" columns I made from a couple of paper towel roll holders. I slit the backs and bent them into the column shape that I was after. These need to go between the boxed in overhanging sides of the fireplace, and the two little bases that have just been glued on. To form the curved parts at the top and base of each column, I used scrunched pieces of newspaper held in shape with masking tape. The columns need to be just in from the sides, exposing some of the plasterwork.

To make the edges of the boxed shaped pieces at the top of the fireplace, I used cut and bent pieces of cardboard. The raised design in the centre I made simply by gluing on a metal finding from my jewellery box, with a ring of metallic twisted braid around it. When this is covered in papier mache the pattern shows through and looks very effective. The metallic braid seems to keep its shape well when covered in papier mache.

With the fireplace in its final position, I had a good look at it to see if it was level and correctly proportioned. I then cut a mantle shelf from single corrugated cardboard to fit snugly on top. This was glued into position and weighted down while it dried to keep it level.

As a stickler for authenticity, I didn't just want to paint on the brickwork inside the chimney breast, but you could do this if you preferred. Or you could simply paint it matt black and blame the maid for not doing her job properly! I worked out the correct size for a brick in the scale I was using, then measured and cut many bricks out of thin card. These in turn were stuck in the correct overlapping brick fashion to the back and sides of the chimney, leaving very small gaps in between for the "rendering". You could stick them onto three pieces of card and then stick the cards inside, if you feel confident that you can join the sides up to look as though it is all one thing.

Quarry tiles

I did the same thing for the quarry tiles on the floor of the hearth. These are square pieces of card, cut and glued down as before.

Floorboards

These are long strips of thin cardboard, glued in place as real floorboards lie.

I covered all the bricks, quarry tiles and floorboards with a layer of tissue. I didn't want to lose any definition and newspaper is too thick. I needed a light covering of paper but obviously didn't want to lose the patterns in doing so. I brushed on some diluted pva glue onto the surface to be covered, then gently laid the tissue pieces on top. When dry the bricks were painted varying shades of reds, pinks and browns. The quarry tiles red tones and the floorboards yellows and browns smudged together. I outlined the bricks and quarry tiles with grey paint to represent cement using a thin paintbrush.

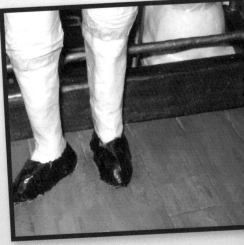

The firegrate

To make the firegrate, I again studied pictures of grates of this era. I chose an Adams firegrate as it would look fitting with the fire surround I had chosen. I did some drawings of the grates and cut pieces of card to the right shape. I couldn't make the grate as deep as they actually were as my hearth is only representative and does not go back very far. However, by accentuating the height of the back of the grate, I was able to give the impression that it actually went back further. I left a gap to fill in later with some "coals".

I am building a Regency dollshouse and I have an Adams fireplace in one of its rooms. I used this is a guide to help me build the papier mache one.

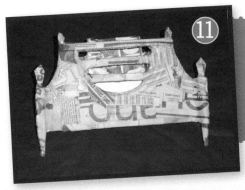

Papier mache strips were placed all over the firegrate, then when dry, I glued on some loops of metallic cord to give a raised pattern on the surface. Another layer was added when the glue had dried then it was left to thoroughly dry out.

I later cut the sides down a little as I wasn't happy with the overall shape.

Adams fireplaces were made of pewter so I used a metallic silver paint, then dry brushed with black ink to get this effect. A few coats of paint and it looked ready for some spit and polish!

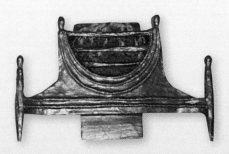

The coals

⑬

You could use all sorts of things to make the coals – pieces of broken black plastic, square beads or painted polystryrene chips. I made mine out of a slab of pulped papier mache to adhere to my paper only agenda. I cut two pieces of thin card first; one for the base (very narrow) and one for the back, to the height I wanted the coals. I held the two pieces together with masking tape and then placed my pulp onto it. The great thing about pulped papier mache is its rough texture when dry. It lends itself to coals quite naturally. You can make the fire look very real by carefully painting it. Deep reds low inside the coals where the heat is blistering, ending with grey tops where the edges of the coals have burnt and turned to ash. You can make the fire blazing or just ticking over.

⑭

The coals were then glued into the firegrate and the whole thing glued into the hearth. In doing this I had to make sure that the back was fully pressed against the bricks and the feet to the floor. You may need to hold it all in position for a while until the glue dries (one of the little pleasures of making dioramas!)

Decorating the fire surround

⑮

With the chimney breast and hearth painted, the firegrate and coals in place, I was ready to paint the surround. White paint was used all over it, then the columns were picked out in varying forms of grey and white paint to represent marble. To make a marble effect, keep your paints on the watery side and lightly brush the different tones onto the surface to be painted, smudging them slightly as you go. Keep the strokes in the same basic direction. When dry, take some white or black paint and a very thin brush and paint tiny veins all travelling in the same direction, but the opposite way to before. A very realistic marble effect can be achieved this way. Marble comes in a multitude of different colours so you can go to town on this. I wanted to keep mine fairly simple on this occasion as I didn't want the colours to clash with or overpower my main subjects. A coat of satin polyurethane varnish over the marbled area was added to help protect it and give it a nice sheen.

Fire Guard

The fire guard I made from thin cardboard. The rails are plastic drinking straws covered in strips of paper that I painted to resemble brass and glued into place.

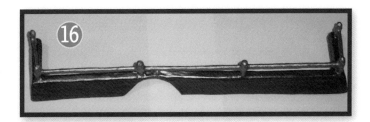

A cut out was made in the fire guard to fit around the cone of cardboard used to make Elizabeth's dress.

Making the figures

With the basic wire armature in hand, I filled out the head and body with pieces of scrunched newspaper taped all round. Be very sparing with this. You can build up the bodies later on, and indeed with the many layers of papier mache you will do just that, so you don't want the figures to look as though they have had too many dinners! Heads are always a problem. As I used pulped papier mache for the heads, I used very little

newspaper inside and kept the wire loop fairly small. If you get the size of the head wrong at this stage it will be hard to correct it later.

For the parts of the body unclothed – faces, arms, hands and in Elizabeth's case, shoulders, I used pulped papier mache made from toilet paper. This very fine paper makes an excellent, almost porcelain looking flesh. I used white toilet paper, but dyed it a flesh colour before mixing in the glue. Don't be temped to use pink coloured paper as this will make them look unreal. The pulp was made in the usual way, but instead of wallpaper paste I used diluted pva.

For full instructions on making realistic skin, see "On To The Arty Bit" – "Skin Deep".

Papier mache mixed with pva adhesive dries much more quickly than wallpaper paste. This is both a help and a hindrance. It allows you to add your layers more quickly, but it practically dries while you look at it and gives you less time to tweak it. However it is well worth doing it this way.

I built up layers, just adding a little at a time. As the figures filled out more I started to build up the features – brows, cheekbones, noses and ears. I constantly referred to my pictures for side and back views. Using discarded dental instruments (these are excellent miniature modelling tools) I used tiny pieces of pulp to make the smallest features like the eyelids and lips. This is a time consuming job and a lot of people might resort to using clay or plaster at this stage, but if you want to make it all out of paper, here is proof that it can be done – if you've got the time and the patience!

As you can imagine, I had to sand the piece after every drying session. Pulp papier mache with pva adhesive is difficult to sand so it took many, many hours to get the finish I required.

As I pre-dyed the pulped tissue paper I had no need to paint the flesh. The only paint I did use was for the eyes, lips and hair. I also gave Elizabeth a blush of pink, and Darcy a bit of stubble!

The hair was also made from the same pulped toilet paper. I wanted to get detail in the form of curls so this was the ideal way to do it. Again, this was a very painstaking practice. Each curl had to be built up slowly over time. The time spent though is well worth it when you see the end results and you will be really proud of yourself.

Dressing the figures

Dressing the figures really is a fun part. Less can go wrong and the lines the clothes lie in is less rigid and there is so much more flexibility. As before, it is very important to study pictures of dress in the chosen period. Note where the waistbands are, how long the coat tails drop and what sort of neckline they wore.

Darcy

Darcy's clothes are made entirely from coloured paper (no painting). I dressed Darcy first as I knew how I wanted him to look; smart in a black jacket over cream coloured breeches. His garters were added first, using white copy paper. I made his breeches in cream coloured craft paper. (Make sure you pad him out in all the right places first!) Where they ended just below his knee, I slid the paper so that it formed creases for a better fit.

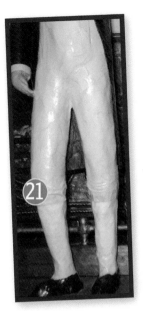

Darcy's shoes and jacket are black paper. I used a piece of thin card to make his coat tail which I also covered in black strips before gluing it to the back of him.

Next I made his shirt. You only need to cover the small area around his neck. The collar I made from a piece of very thin card, glued around his neck and covered it with the same white paper. For his neck tie I used a short piece of florists crumpled crepe paper (the sort they use to make huge bows around bunches of flowers).

His waistcoat is simply made from kitchen paper. If you want to do something similar, look for one that has a suitable impressed pattern or use plain.

Darcy's jacket is made from a thick black paper. When using thick paper like this, you don't want to be overlapping the pieces too much, or the figure will become too large.

Elizabeth

A cone of cardboard formed the main part of Elizabeth's dress. The top of the cardboard came right up to just under her bust as was the fashion then. For the dress I used some very good quality rose coloured tissue paper, the type that doesn't run when it gets wet. Tissue is a very good representation of silk. For the sleeves and bodice, I cut small pieces of tissue as though I was making them out of material. The long drapes of the dress are concertinered at the back to give fullness behind her. As she is standing so near to the fireguard, I softly draped her skirt over the grate to add more interest.

The tissue was glued on with pva glue. When it was thoroughly dry, I coated it with several more coats of pva to protect and stiffen the tissue.

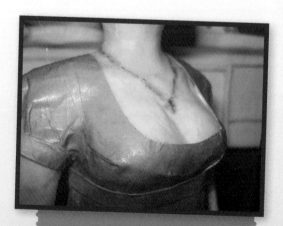

Elizabeth's gloves and necklace are painted on.

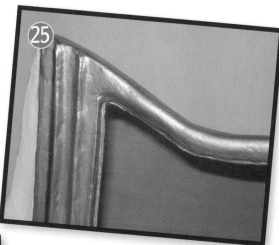

Backing Board

I had a real glass mirror cut in a wavy pattern for the mirror above the fireplace. (There is no paper substitute that can simulate glass, that I know of!) I built up a frame all around it with pulped papier mache. It took an enormous amount of sanding to get it smooth and rounded. After the emulsion coats, I painted it with gold acrylic paint.

Candlesticks

These I made from plastic straws, with varying sizes of circular cardboard discs, placed at strategic points along the straws. A small piece of twisted newspaper formed the candles. I used very small pieces of pasted paper to cover the tiny shapes.

Painted in silver metallic paint, with white for the candles, these were then glued to the fireplace.

Fire Iron

This fire iron (or poker) I made in a similar way to the candlesticks, a plastic straw with a cardboard disc and knob of papier mache to form the handle.

㉗

Pots

I didn't use any mould or form to make these pots. I simply made them from a tightly squashed ball of pasted newspaper, teased into a rough pot shape. A round piece of card was used for the base of the lid and a tiny ball of paper for the handle knob. I left the pots for a very long time to dry out, then using a sharp craft knife, I literally carved the shape of the pots to how I wanted them to look.

㉘

I painted one design on the front of each pot.

An alternative design for the back of the pot was painted to cast a reflection in the mirror.

These were fun to paint and I based them on some antique pots that I had sourced pictures of.

Clock

To make the clock, I cut a chunk of polystyrene the size that I wanted the clock to be. I carved out a shape that was flat back and front, with protruding edges at the top and slightly longer at the base. I looked through all my antique books to look at clocks from around the Regency period. I couldn't find exactly what I was looking for, as I wanted a really elaborate clock. I used my artist's licence and made my own version out of ideas from several different clocks.

I covered the polystyrene with some very small strips of papier mache just to cover it completely and give me a nice base to stick pulp onto to form the decoration.

I wanted pillars (two each side) and this was easy to achieve by using four cut down cocktail sticks, wrapped around in a narrow pasted paper strip.

Toilet paper pulp was used as in the figures. I made twisty shapes of it down the pillars and tiny flowers and leaves on the front and top of the face. Starting off with a small mound of pulp on the top of the clock, I moulded it into a tiny cherub with wings. As with the faces of Elizabeth and Darcy, it took a lot of patience building up the tiny features and waiting for it to dry in between.

For the clock face, I cut a picture out of a magazine and glued this on the front. This way I was still sticking to my paper only theme.

 The painting was very intricate and I had to use a magnifying glass to get it right. The gold pillars, wings and random highlights amongst the flowers and leaves made it look like a classy item.

Dog

I didn't think the scene would be complete without a small dog at Elizabeth's feet, as it was very common for Regency women to keep them.

I chose a King Charles Spaniel. I borrowed a china ornament of one of this breed of dogs and used it as my guide. The ornament was smaller than the one I wanted to make, but it gave me a good idea of what the dog would look like from all angles.

(31)

I built up layers over small pieces of cardboard. I placed papier mache over the whole dog then painted it white. Where I was not happy with the way he was looking, I took out a sharp craft knife and trimmed him into shape.

The finished papier mache dog with his china counterpart.

The features were painted on when he was dry and I brushed him with a diluted pva coat to protect him. It gave him a soft sheen, but these dogs have quite silky coats so it looked about right.

Chapter 20

Where To Go
From Here

I hope you have enjoyed following my experiences with art & design in papier mache. It really is such fun to design your own work. It is extremely satisfying knowing that you have come up with your own unique ideas.

Inspiration is all around us and sometimes we are just too busy to see. Trees and plants, shapes and colours, even reflections and shadows are all worth observing and can give us ideas on subjects to use in our art.

Just lock the front door and get yourself into a relaxed frame of mind. Put some music on if it helps you. I actually prefer silence when I'm working as I find music (especially the radio!) chimes in on my thoughts.

Make yourself as nice a work area as you can and get a comfortable chair. Forget the outside world and try to put all your troubles to the back of your mind. Devote your thoughts solely to what you have in front of you. Your subconscious will take over and the ideas will start to flow.

If you get to a stage where you are not sure how to proceed – stop! Clear your table and throw away any bits of discarded paper, leaving a nice neat work area. Place your item in a different position, preferably even in a different room, and observe it as you pass it by during the day. Leave it for several days if you like. Then take another good look at it and you will most likely be able to see the way forward. It may mean altering it slightly by cutting it down a bit or building it up in some areas. Never struggle on with a piece just to finish it. You will be disappointed with the results if you do.

When you have created a few pieces, why not show your work on my website: The Papier Mache Resource (http://www.papiermache.co.uk)? Just request your own gallery – it's free! There is a forum on the site and there are many talented and friendly people willing to help you with any papier mache related problems. You could of course just chat about what you are making. You will also find lots more inspiration from many other artists in the galleries.

Happy papier mache designing!